# TOEFL® MAP
## Speaking

**New TOEFL® Edition**

Advanced

**DARAKWON**

# TOEFL® MAP

**New TOEFL® Edition**

## Speaking Advanced

**Publisher** Chung Kyudo
**Editor** Cho Sangik
**Authors** Shane Spivey, Jonathan S. McClelland
**Proofreader** Michael A. Putlack
**Designers** Park Narae, Park Bohee, Chung Kyuok

First published in March 2023
By Darakwon, Inc.
Darakwon Bldg., 211, Munbal-ro, Paju-si, Gyeonggi-do 10881
Republic of Korea
Tel: 82-2-736-2031 (Ext. 250)
Fax: 82-2-732-2037

**Price** ₩19,000
**ISBN** 978-89-277-8036-6 14740
       978-89-277-8025-0 14740 (set)

**www.darakwon.co.kr**

**Photo Credits**
Shutterstock.com

**Components** Main Book / Scripts and Answer Key
7 6 5 4 3 2 1        23 24 25 26 27

# Introduction

Studying for the TOEFL® iBT is no easy task and is not one that is to be undertaken lightly. It requires a great deal of effort as well as dedication on the part of the student. It is our hope that by using *TOEFL® Map Speaking Advanced* as either a textbook or a study guide, the task of studying for the TOEFL® iBT will become somewhat easier for the student and less of a burden.

Students who wish to excel on the TOEFL® iBT must attain a solid grasp of the four important skills in the English language: reading, listening, speaking, and writing. The Darakwon *TOEFL® Map* series covers all four of these skills in separate books. There are also three different levels in all four topics. This book, *TOEFL® Map Speaking Advanced*, covers the speaking aspect of the test at the advanced level. Students who want to listen to lectures and conversations, read academic passages, learn vocabulary and expressions, and study topics that appear on the TOEFL® iBT will be able to do all of these things with this book.

*TOEFL® Map Speaking Advanced* has been designed for use both in a classroom setting and as a study guide for individual learners. For this reason, it offers a comprehensive overview of the TOEFL® iBT Speaking section. In Part A, the different types of questions found on the TOEFL® iBT Speaking section are explained, and students can pick up tips to ensure superior performance, such as things to avoid when preparing an answer. In Part B-1, learners will face actual passages, lectures, and conversations as they would appear on the TOEFL® iBT. They will able to listen to model responses, which provide guidance in formulating their own answers, before giving their own responses. Part B-1 also features ideas and critical thinking questions to jog students' imaginations. In Part B-2, students will have more exposure to actual TOEFL® iBT material as well as the opportunity to use a scoring grid to rate their responses. Finally, in Part C, students can take two TOEFL® iBT practice tests. Combined, each of these elements will help learners prepare themselves to take and, more importantly, excel on the TOEFL® iBT.

*TOEFL® Map Speaking Advanced* has been designed with all aspects of the student's performance in mind. The material found in these pages can prepare students to approach the TOEFL® iBT confidently and to achieve superior results. However, despite the valuable information within this book, nothing can replace a student's own hard work and dedication. In order to maximize the benefits of studying *TOEFL® Map Speaking Advanced*, the student must strive to do his or her best on every task in every chapter. We wish you luck in your study of both English and the TOEFL® iBT, and we hope that you are able to use *TOEFL® Map Speaking Advanced* to improve your abilities in both.

Shane Spivey
Jonathan S. McClelland

# TABLE OF CONTENTS

## Part A | Understanding Speaking Question Types

## Part B-1 | Building Knowledge & Skills for the Speaking Test

# Part B-2 | Mastering Knowledge & Skills for the Speaking Test

# Part C | Experiencing the TOEFL iBT Actual Tests

# How Is This Book Different?

*TOEFL® Map Speaking Advanced* prepares students for success on the TOEFL® iBT with a unique curriculum that can be found in Part B-1 and Part B-2. In Part B-1, students are provided with plenty of ideas and critical thinking questions designed to assist them in developing a logical and organized response to each prompt as well as a sample response to help them model their own response. In Part B-2, students are given less guidance with the chance to apply the skills they learned in Part B-1. A sample response is provided after the student's response. Both sections are filled with useful features to help students develop their critical thinking and organizational abilities.

The primary emphasis of *TOEFL® Map Speaking Advanced* is on invoking ideas. In order to be successful in TOEFL®, especially on the independent speaking tasks, students must learn to conjure ideas quickly and strategically expand them into a complete response. *TOEFL® Map Speaking Advanced* addresses this need with the Idea Box, which is an improvement on the idea web commonly found in TOEFL® iBT Speaking books. While idea webs leave students with several blanks and very little assistance in filling in the blanks, the Idea Box contains questions and statements to help jog students' mind and to develop well-rounded responses to the prompt.

The second unique feature of *TOEFL® Map Speaking Advanced* is that its format provides students the opportunity to gain an in-depth understanding of each question type. The tasks on the TOEFL® iBT Speaking test can be confusing, but with *TOEFL® Map Speaking Advanced*, students will understand each question with complete clarity. The following unique features of this book, found in Part B-1 and Part B-2, help accomplish that goal.

## Sample Response

Each task in the book includes a sample response that can be used as a benchmark for a perfect answer. This response shows students what a perfect response should look like, but students should understand that a high-scoring response can include some errors in pronunciation, diction, and factuality.

## Analyzing

After reading and listening to the sample response, students will locate transitions in the response. This helps students develop awareness of how transitions can be used.

## Deducing

Based on the sample response, students will use inference and information in the response to predict the details of the listening and, when applicable, reading. This skill is useful as a way for students to critically evaluate what they read and hear on the test.

## Prediction

Students will attempt to predict the content of the listening portion of tasks 2 and 3 after reading the accompanying passage. This helps students establish possible contexts for the listening, which eases the difficulty and the tension of hearing a listening passage for the first time.

*TOEFL® Map Speaking Advanced* also places a strong emphasis on critical thinking. The TOEFL® iBT speaking test requires strong analytical skills from the test taker, and this book will help prepare students for that. Each unique feature of this book is designed to promote critical thinking. These questions are designed to help students consider various perspectives of a situation. Not only will this help students develop their own responses to a prompt, but it will also jump-start their creativity and ability to respond in class.

Some tasks in the book contain questions about the material that should be answered with a brief spoken response. This helps students warm up before delivering their actual response to the prompt.

Finally, students and teachers will be delighted with the scoring grids, which appear in every task of Part B-2 in *TOEFL® Map Speaking Advanced*. Teachers can use this scoring grid in several ways: to score the students' responses, to have students score their own responses, or to have students score other students' responses. Using the scoring grid will give students an intimate understanding of the TOEFL® iBT Speaking scoring rubric, and it will help them internalize the factors that make up a strong response. Most importantly, it will allow students to see exactly which areas of their performance require the most attention.

# How to Use This Book

*TOEFL® Map Speaking Advanced* was designed with each component in mind to specifically hone students' skills. The material progresses from Part B-1 with plenty of guidance to assist students in developing their responses, to Part B-2 with less guidance and more critical thinking, to Part C with two actual tests that offer no assistance.

Teachers are encouraged to use the book from start to finish. Students should follow the directions presented for each task and skip none of the tasks. This method will provide the most benefit to students in terms of both their speaking ability and test-taking ability.

Before beginning Part B-1 of the book, teachers may wish to review the TOEFL® iBT Speaking scoring rubric with students. That rubric is provided on page 27. It is crucial that students understand the rubric before using the scoring grids in Part B-2.

## Part A Understanding Speaking Question Types

This section is designed to acquaint students with the types of questions found on the TOEFL® iBT Speaking test. Each question, called a "task," is fully explained so that students can understand which abilities the task specifically tests and what kind of response should be given. Students can also see example tasks and responses and pick up helpful tips that will enable them to succeed on each task. It is critical that students and teachers familiarize themselves with the information found in Part A before moving to Part B-1.

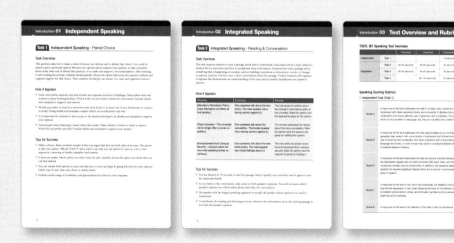

# Part B-1 Building Knowledge & Skills for the Speaking Test

## Independent Speaking Task 1

The purpose of this section is to give students guidance on how to master the independent speaking task. Students will make use of the questions and the ideas provided to help them formulate and develop effective responses to the prompts. The specific exercises are as follows:

## Planning

This exercise has been designed to provide maximum assistance to students.
On Task 1, students should use the Idea Box to prepare an answer for both choices, which will foster greater critical thinking.

## Speaking

Students should give a response to the prompt as they would on the test.
The Transitions and Canned Phrases section can be used to guide students as they speak.

## Comparing

Students finally listen to a sample response to the prompt. Students are advised to pay attention to the content and organization of the response and to compare it with their own.

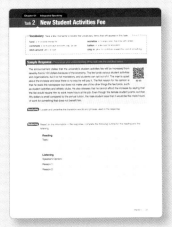

## Integrated Speaking Task 2 & 3

In tasks 2 and 3 of Part B-1, students begin by listening to and reading a sample response. This provides the basis for the goals for this section, which are to familiarize students with an appropriate answer format and to help students critically analyze written and spoken information. Students then read and listen to the passage and conversation/lecture for the task, warm up with some brief speaking, and complete the task. More information on the exercises for tasks 2 and 3 is provided below.

## Sample Response

A sample response appears before the reading and listening portions of each task. Students should read and listen to the response and analyze the transitions used by the speaker. Students then use critical thinking to infer the details of the written and spoken information in the task.

## Reading

Students read the passage as it would appear on the test. Following the passage are questions designed to check comprehension, to promote critical thinking, and to allow students to warm up before giving their response to the prompt.

## Listening

The conversation or lecture is played as students take notes. On task 2, students are told which speaker's opinion to note. This differs from the actual TOEFL® iBT Speaking test and has been designed as special assistance for the purposes of practice and training. In Part B-2, students do not have this advantage.

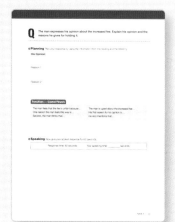

## Planning

Students should pull together all of the information from the sample response, the reading, and the listening to plan their own response.

## Speaking

Students should respond to the prompt in the given time and use the Transitions and Canned Phrases section as necessary.

## Integrated Speaking Task 4

The purpose of this section is to give students a comprehensive understanding of task 4. The task begins with a sample response that students can evaluate and imitate. Through a series of exercises detailed below, students work their way to the end of the task to finally giving their own response to the prompt.

## Sample Response

A sample response appears before the listening portion of the task in order to prepare students for the information presented in the lecture. Students should read and listen to the response, analyze it to determine how it uses transitions, and use it infer the contents of the listening.

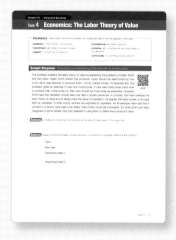

## Listening

Students have already deduced the information from the listening portion by reading the sample response, so notes should be kept to a minimum. Students should focus on listening for additional details.

## Planning

Students can use the information from the sample response and the listening to plan their own response to the prompt.

## Speaking

Students use their plan to give a response. The Transitions and Canned Phrases section can be used as a guide to help move from the introduction to the details.

# Part B-2 Mastering Knowledge & Skills for the Speaking Test

## Independent Speaking Task 1

The first task appears differently in Part B-2. Students are provided with minimal guidance and are expected to put to practice the critical-thinking skills developed in Part B-1. In the independent task, students will read the prompt and directly plan their answers before making use of the other exercises found in this section.

## Tip

This is the only guidance provided to students in the independent task in Part B-2. Students should read the tip and consider how it can help them generate more critical-analysis questions and, ultimately, more ideas for their response.

## Planning

A basic outline, which students can use to organize their own response, has been provided.

## Speaking

Here, students compile the information from the speaking plan and give their responses to the prompt. The Transitions and Canned Phrases section can be used as a guide for speaking.

## Grading

The final exercise consists of speaking and listening. Students hear a sample response and have the opportunity to use the scoring chart to measure their own performance on the task. The scoring chart can provide useful insight into the elements of a perfect response and highlight each student's individual problem areas.

## Integrated Speaking Task 2 & 3

This section provides students with less guidance than in Part B-1 and puts more of an emphasis on critical thinking and analysis. Students should take advantage of the following exercises to maximize their potential on tasks 2 and 3 of the TOEFL® iBT Speaking test.

## Reading

The passage appears as it would on the test. Students read the passage in the allotted time and take notes. Afterward, students predict the content of the listening and answer a critical-thinking question.

## Listening

Students listen to the conversation or lecture and take notes on the important information and details within each. Students then critically analyze the listening passage in order to check their comprehension and to ensure they have a complete understanding of the reading and the listening as a whole.

## Planning

Here, students should organize the information from the reading and the listening to organize and plan their own response.

## Speaking

Based on the information in the speaking plan, students give their timed response to the prompt. The Transitions and Canned Phrases section can be consulted as needed.

## Grading

Students should listen to a sample four-point response after giving their own response to the prompt. After considering both, students or teachers may use the scoring chart to grade students' responses. This allows both teachers and students to target specific areas that students need to improve.

## Integrated Speaking Task 4

The final integrated task offers little guidance to students and instead emphasize critical thinking and evaluation of the material. Students are presented with a lecture as it would appear on the test. After answering some critical-thinking questions about the material, students deliver their responses and use the scoring grid. Each exercise is explained in more detail below.

## Listening

Students hear the lecture and take notes as they listen. Following the listening, two critical-analysis questions help students deepen their understanding of the listening material and develop concepts for their responses.

## Planning

Students follow the outline notes provided to plan their response for the task's question.

## Speaking

Students give their response based on the allotted time frame for the task. They may refer to the Transitions and Canned Phrases section as they speak.

## Grading

Students can hear a sample four-point response to the prompt. Students should use this opportunity to spot areas of their own response that need improvement. The scoring chart allows teachers or fellow students to evaluate students' responses. The scoring chart is a critical tool for gaining insight into the criteria used to grade responses on the TOEFL® iBT Speaking test.

# Part C Experiencing the TOEFL iBT Actual Tests

This final portion of the book gives students a chance to experience an actual TOEFL® iBT test. There are two sets of tests that are modeled on the Speaking section of the TOEFL® iBT. The topics are similar to those on the real test, as are the questions. Taking these tests allows students the opportunity to measure their own performance ability on an actual test.

# Part

# A

# Understanding Speaking Question Types

## Task 1 | Independent Speaking - Paired Choice

## Task Overview

This question asks you to make a choice between two options and to defend that choice. You could be asked to give a personal opinion between two options and to support your opinion, to take a position about some issue and to defend that position, or to make and support a recommendation. After listening to and reading the prompt, students should quickly choose the option that seems the easiest to defend and organize support for that choice. Then, students should give an answer in a clear and organized manner.

## How It Appears

- Some universities separate men and women into separate dormitory buildings. Others allow men and women to share housing facilities. Which policy do you think is better for universities? Include details and examples to support your answer.

- Would you prefer to study at a university near your home or to move out of your hometown or country to study? Using details and examples, explain which you would prefer and why.

- Is it important for students to have access to the latest technology? Use details and examples to support your opinion.

- Some people enjoy listening to music when they study. Others think it is better to study in silence. Which do you prefer and why? Include details and examples to support your answer.

## Tips for Success

- ○ Make a choice. Many students wonder if they can argue that they see both sides of an issue. The answer is that you cannot. Official TOEFL® raters want to see that you can defend an opinion with a clear argument consisting of details, examples, and reasons.

- ○ It does not matter which option you select from the pair. Quickly choose the option you think that you can best defend.

- ○ You can restate both options in your introduction, or you can begin by going directly into your opinion. Either way, be sure that your choice is clearly stated.

- ○ Include a wide range of vocabulary and grammatical structures in your response.

# Task Example

## ⊘ Question

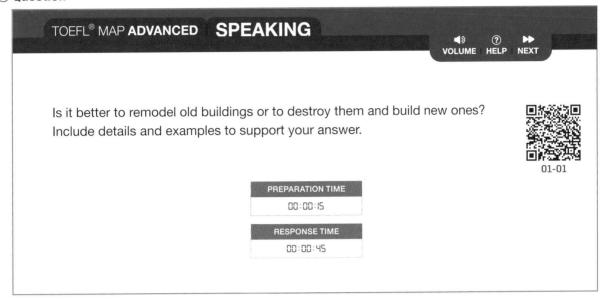

TOEFL® MAP **ADVANCED** **SPEAKING**

◄) VOLUME ⓘ HELP ► NEXT

Is it better to remodel old buildings or to destroy them and build new ones? Include details and examples to support your answer.

01-01

PREPARATION TIME
00:00:15

RESPONSE TIME
00:00:45

## ⊘ Sample Response

**Introduction**  In my opinion, it is better to keep old buildings and to restore them than to destroy them to make room for new buildings.

**Detail 1**  The main reason I feel this way is that old buildings add a sense of history. In my hometown, there are some old houses that were built in the 1800s. Even though no one lives in them anymore, the local government pays to keep them in good condition. People around town love having a glimpse of the past.

**Detail 2**  I also believe that maintaining old buildings gives better variety. Older architectural styles are different from newer designs, so having a mix of buildings from different eras prevents the monotony of similar-looking buildings and gives people more choices about what type of building they wish to rent or buy.

## ⊘ Explanation

A four-point response to the first task should be one that clearly takes a side and defends it well. In this task, the student is asked to give an opinion about an issue. The sample response begins with a thesis statement that directly states the speaker's opinion. The two supporting details are not mentioned in the introduction to save time for elaboration. The signal words that lead into each supporting detail ("The main reason I feel this way" and "I also believe") create a clear structure in the response. The first detail is supported with an example that explains the reason. The second detail is supported with an argument.

## Task 2 | Integrated Speaking - Reading & Conversation

### Task Overview

This task requires students to read a passage about and to understand a discussion about a topic related to student life at a university and then to paraphrase some information. Students first read a passage about something that is happening on campus, such as building renovations or relocations, events, or changes to policies. Students will then hear a short conversation about the passage. Finally, students will organize a response that demonstrates an understanding of the topic and accurately paraphrases one speaker's opinion.

### How It Appears

| Reading | Listening | Prompt |
|---|---|---|
| [Mandatory Attendance Policy – Class attendance will affect all final grades.] | [Two speakers talk about the new policy. The male speaker has a strong opinion against it.] | The man gives his opinion about the change in attendance policy at the university. State his opinion and the reasons he gives for his opinion. |
| [Class Canceled – The university will no longer offer a course on pottery.] | [Two speakers talk about the cancelation. The female speaker has a strong opinion against it.] | The woman expresses her opinion about the class cancelation. State her opinion and the reasons she gives for holding that opinion. |
| [Announcement from Campus Security – Campus police will now write speeding tickets on campus.] | [Two speakers talk about the new ticket policy. The male speaker has mixed feelings about it.] | The man gives his opinion about the announcement from campus security. State his opinion and the reasons he gives for holding it. |

### Tips for Success

○ You are allowed 45-50 seconds to read the passage. Read it quickly once and then read it again to note the important details.

○ As you listen to the conversation, take notes on both speakers' opinions. You will not know which speaker's opinion you will be asked about until after the conversation.

○ The speaker with the longest speaking segments is usually the speaker whose opinion you need to summarize.

○ To synthesize the reading and listening portions, reference the information from the reading passage as you state the speaker's opinion.

# Task Example

## ⊘ Reading

City University's Dean of Academic Affairs has decided to institute a mandatory attendance policy. Read the announcement from the dean. You will have 45 seconds to read the announcement. Begin reading now.

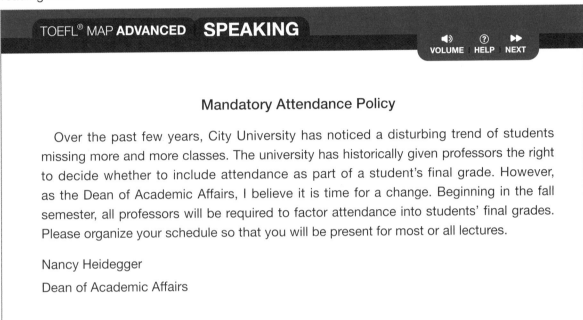

TOEFL® MAP **ADVANCED** **SPEAKING**

◀) VOLUME | ⑦ HELP | ▶▶ NEXT

### Mandatory Attendance Policy

Over the past few years, City University has noticed a disturbing trend of students missing more and more classes. The university has historically given professors the right to decide whether to include attendance as part of a student's final grade. However, as the Dean of Academic Affairs, I believe it is time for a change. Beginning in the fall semester, all professors will be required to factor attendance into students' final grades. Please organize your schedule so that you will be present for most or all lectures.

Nancy Heidegger
Dean of Academic Affairs

## ⊘ Listening

Now listen to two students as they discuss the announcement.

M: Oh, my. I can't believe the university is actually doing this.

W: I don't know what you're so upset about. Surely this is for the best. Students ought to attend class.

M: Not always. Many professors acknowledge that attendance of a lecture isn't crucial for digesting the course material. That's why they don't require attendance.

W: What are you getting at?

M: Well, the dean seems to think she knows more than the professors. She's taking away their freedom as educators to decide how to run their classes.

W: I see what you mean.

M: And not only that, but now classes will be packed with apathetic students. I kind of like it when those students don't come to class. That way, the classroom is filled with people who want to be there and not anyone who is annoyed or falling asleep.

W: I'm not sure how this benefits you.

M: It benefits everyone because we can have better class discussions. Having apathetic students in class will just slow down the tempo of the lectures and the discussions.

01-02

## ⊘ Question

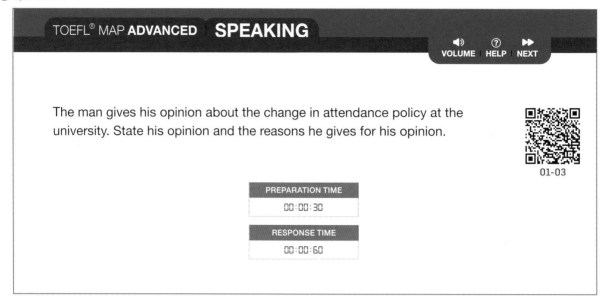

TOEFL® MAP **ADVANCED**  **SPEAKING**

◀ VOLUME | ⓘ HELP | ▶▶ NEXT

The man gives his opinion about the change in attendance policy at the university. State his opinion and the reasons he gives for his opinion.

01-03

PREPARATION TIME

00:00:30

RESPONSE TIME

00:00:60

## ⊘ Sample Response

Introduction  The students are reacting to an announcement about the new attendance policy, which will require attendance to be a part of students' final grades. The man is upset about the new policy for two reasons.

Detail 1  He begins by arguing that the change takes freedoms away from the professors. In the past, professors have been free to decide if students need to attend. The man says this is good because some classes do not necessarily require lecture attendance for students to grasp the material. With the change, professors will no longer be able to structure their classes the way they want to.

Detail 2  The man then states that he feels the new policy will reduce the quality of the lectures. He says that students who don't go to lectures are apathetic. He's glad they don't go to class because they can't contribute to the discussions. With the new policy, though, the man worries that the lectures will be slowed down by students who aren't interested in the material.

## ⊘ Explanation

The second task requires that the student understand one speaker's opinion in relation to the reading passage. This requires the student to summarize and to paraphrase. The sample response begins with an introduction that neatly summarizes the topic of discussion. The introduction also states the thesis statement that the man is upset with the new policy. Using signal words ("He begins by" and "The man then states"), the student moves into the first point of the man's argument, which is paraphrased in detail. The speaker then moves onto the second reason and presents an equally organized and accurate paraphrasing of the man's opinion.

## Task Overview

This task asks students to read a passage that gives general information about an academic topic and to understand a lecture that provides details on the topic. The topic can be from practically any major field of academic study. After reading the passage, students will listen to part of a lecture. The lecture usually contains two supporting details, which may be arguments, descriptions of specific categories or types, reasons for a phenomenon, examples, or personal experience anecdotes. Finally, students will explain the lecture information with reference to the reading passage.

## How It Appears

| Reading | Listening | Prompt |
|---|---|---|
| [Bird Flight Mechanisms – Information about two ways that birds fly] | [The lecture explains both methods of flying in greater detail.] | The professor explains flight mechanisms in birds. Describe the methods that birds use to fly. |
| [Employee Motivation – A summary of motivation techniques used by managers] | [The professor gives information about a specific technique and relates a personal story to explain it.] | The professor explains one management technique for motivating employees. Describe this technique and how it is used to motivate employees. |
| [Sports Injuries – A description of common injuries suffered by athletes] | [The lecture introduces the topic and gives details about two common injuries.] | The professor explains how athletes can become injured while playing sports. Describe the injuries and how they occur. |

## Tips for Success

○ Take notes on the main idea and any important details while you read.

○ Determine the relationship of the lecture to the reading passage. Does the lecture go into greater detail about a topic? Does it argue against the topic? Does it give examples of categories mentioned in the passage?

○ The reading passage often expresses an abstract concept. In this case, be prepared for the lecture to present concrete examples to illustrate the concept.

○ Listen for signal words in the lecture. These will help you organize your notes.

# Task Example

## ⊘ Reading

Read the passage about the War of 1812. You have 45 seconds to read the passage. Begin reading now.

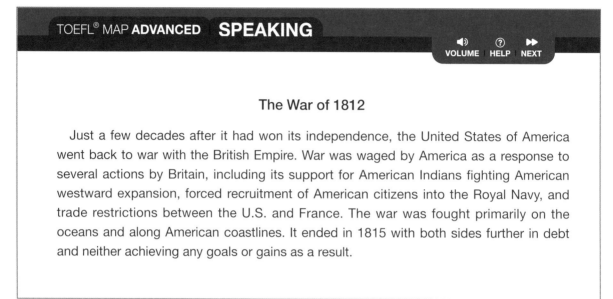

### The War of 1812

Just a few decades after it had won its independence, the United States of America went back to war with the British Empire. War was waged by America as a response to several actions by Britain, including its support for American Indians fighting American westward expansion, forced recruitment of American citizens into the Royal Navy, and trade restrictions between the U.S. and France. The war was fought primarily on the oceans and along American coastlines. It ended in 1815 with both sides further in debt and neither achieving any goals or gains as a result.

## ⊘ Listening

Now listen to part of a lecture on the same topic in a history class.

**Professor (Male)**

In many ways, the War of 1812 was a war to change feelings and opinions than anything else. It was an important war but not necessarily for its apparent causes and effects.

Let's talk first about what started the war. Sure, there were claimed factors such as British restrictions on trade and requiring American citizens to serve in the Royal Navy, but that doesn't get to the root of why America went to war. Many historians maintain that declaring war was a way for the U.S. to gain respect in the face of the empire. How dare the British recruit our citizens for their navy and tell us who we can trade with?

By the end of the war, most of the original reasons for war were moot since the British were no longer at war with France. A treaty was finally signed in which neither side really gained much in the way of measurable or tangible results. But what was gained was a new respect for the U.S. Americans claimed the war a second victorious war of independence while many British began to look at the U.S. as a respectable, independent nation.

## ⊘ Question

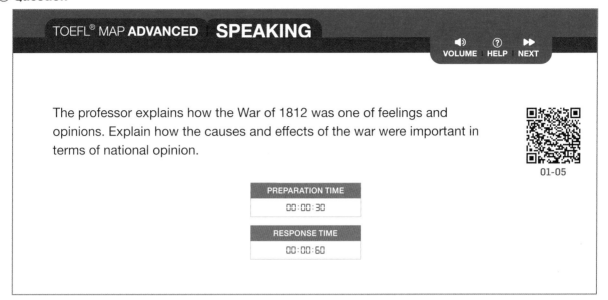

The professor explains how the War of 1812 was one of feelings and opinions. Explain how the causes and effects of the war were important in terms of national opinion.

01-05

PREPARATION TIME

00:00:30

RESPONSE TIME

00:00:60

## ⊘ Sample Response

**Introduction**  The War of 1812 was a three-year war between the U.S. and the British Empire. It was started because of actions by the British that interfered with American goals, such as helping Native Americans fight the U.S. and blocking trade with France.

**Detail 1**  The professor explains that the war had more to do with feelings and opinions than with actual causes of war. He states that Americans viewed the actions of the British with contempt. By doing such things as restricting trade, Britain did not treat America as an independent nation. That's why the U.S. went to war: to earn respect from the empire.

**Detail 2**  The professor continues his argument by looking at the results of the war. There were no measurable gains by either side. The real gain was for the United States. Its own citizens felt more pride as a result of its second resistance of the British Empire's might, and, likewise, the British developed a newfound respect for the new country.

## ⊘ Explanation

The goal of the third task is to show that students are able to synthesize material from written and spoken sources. Student responses must accurately convey important information from both sources. In the sample response, the student begins by giving a summary of the reading passage. The student then moves directly into the passage's correlation with the lecture by explaining the professor's opinion about the War of 1812. The response summarizes the first point of the lecture, regarding the emotional motivations of the war. Using a clear transition ("The professor continues his argument by"), the student then paraphrases the second point of the lecture. No important details are missing from the response.

## Task Overview

This task consists of a lecture about an academic topic. The topic can be from virtually any major field of academic study, but it focuses on a detailed aspect of that field. The lecture is usually divided into an introduction and two supporting details. The passage does not expect students to have knowledge of technical terminology, but it is assumed that students will possess an advanced vocabulary. After hearing the lecture, students will summarize its content.

## How It Appears

| Listening | Prompt |
| --- | --- |
| [The lecture is about Japanese and German causes of World War II.] | Using points and examples from the lecture, explain how Japanese and German activities led to the start of World War II. |
| [The lecture gives information about two reasons dogs are bred.] | Using points and examples from the lecture, explain the purpose of dog breeding. |
| [The professor explains the role of bicycles in the early feminist movement in the U.S.] | Using points and examples from the lecture, explain what role bicycles played in the early American feminist movement. |

## Tips for Success

○ Listen for words that the professor emphasizes as well as any technical terms and vocabulary. Write them down and include them in your summary.

○ Organize your note paper into two sections: main idea and details. While listening, circle any words that you feel are key words to be included in your response.

○ One of the greatest challenges for students in this task is accurately and completely presenting the facts. It is imperative that you develop strong note-taking skills. Abbreviate long words and use mathematical symbols to replace transition or linking words.

○ The professor does not always give strong signal words to separate ideas. As you listen, take notes in a linear fashion and try to establish the lecture's organization as you listen.

# Task Example

## ⊘ Listening

Listen to part of a lecture in a fine arts class.

### Professor (Female)

01-06

When you think of pop art, what's the first thing that comes to mind? Probably the image of a Campbell's soup can, right? But what does it mean? What is pop art? Well, first we need to understand the origins of the movement.

In the 1950s, a bunch of artists calling themselves the Independent Group, or IG, met in London to discuss modernist art. Members of the IG noticed the increased sophistication of American commercial art and wondered why the art world considered it low brow. They saw great value in commercial art and, well, wanted to display it as fine art. At their first meeting, artists presented their works of collages, composed mostly of images found in magazines, comic books, and that kind of thing. The works were, for the most part, unaltered, with the images presented "as is" to the viewer.

Many say the movement truly began in the U.S. It traveled across the Atlantic in the 1960s, and this is when it really took off. Artists in the States took to it differently from their British counterparts. See, uh, the British artists looked at American mass media from the outside, so they saw it as charming and maybe even a bit romantic. American artists, though, were constantly confronted with advertising and commercial art on a daily basis. When they began making pop art in the '60s, the motivation wasn't really to glorify commercial art; The point was to take these images out of context. By putting a soup can in a picture frame, it becomes cold and impersonal. American pop artists wanted to draw parallels between mass-produced products and people.

## ⊘ Question

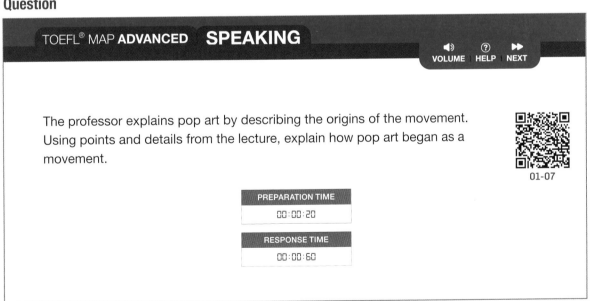

The professor explains pop art by describing the origins of the movement. Using points and details from the lecture, explain how pop art began as a movement.

01-07

**PREPARATION TIME**
00:00:20

**RESPONSE TIME**
00:00:60

## ⊚ Sample Response

Introduction    The lecture focuses on the topic of pop art, specifically how it got its start in England and the United States.

Detail 1    The professor begins the lecture by talking about a group of artists in England called the Independent Group. They met to discuss art of their day, and they were in disagreement with most art critics, who said that commercial art was low brow. They thought the art deserved to be appreciated for its own merits, so they created collages using pictures of commercial art they found in print media.

Detail 2    After its beginnings in England, the new art form, pop art, traveled to the United States over the next decade. But, the professor explains, the American artists had a different view of commercial art. They did not see it as romantic or praiseworthy as the British artists did. Instead, they wanted to show that commercial art was mass-produced imagery and that that was how we as humans were becoming because of mass production.

## ⊚ Explanation

The fourth task calls on students to summarize the information in a lecture. Students must be sure to repeat the information as accurately and completely as possible. The sample response to this prompt begins with an introduction that contains a brief summary of the lecture's main idea. Using a clear transition to indicate the start of the first detail ("The professor begins by"), the response summarizes the first detail and describes it accurately and fully. The response transitions into the second detail of the lecture and finishes with a strong paraphrasing of the pop art movement in the United States.

## TOEFL iBT Speaking Test Overview

| | | Reading | Listening | Preparation | Response |
|---|---|---|---|---|---|
| Independent | Task 1 | | | 15 seconds | 45 seconds |
| Integrated | Task 2 | 45-50 seconds | 60-80 seconds | 30 seconds | 60 seconds |
| | Task 3 | 45-50 seconds | 60-90 seconds | 30 seconds | 60 seconds |
| | Task 4 | | 60-120 seconds | 20 seconds | 60 seconds |

## Speaking Scoring Rubrics

### 1. Independent Task (Task 1)

| Score 4 | A response at this level addresses the task in a highly clear, sustained manner. It is well developed with ideas explained clearly and coherently. It displays fluid speech that is easy to understand and shows effective use of grammar and vocabulary. Though it may have minor errors in pronunciation or language use, they do not affect the overall intelligibility or meaning. |
|---|---|
| Score 3 | A response at this level addresses the task appropriately but is not fully developed. It displays generally clear speech with some fluidity of expression and shows somewhat effective use of grammar and vocabulary. But minor problems with pronunciation, pace of speech, language structures, or word choice may result in occasional listener effort to understand and occasional lapses in fluency. |
| Score 2 | A response at this level addresses the task but shows a limited development of ideas. Ideas are expressed vaguely and not well connected with each other, and the use of grammar and vocabulary remains only at a basic level. In addition, the response displays basically clear speech but requires significant listener effort due to errors in pronunciation, intonation, or pace of speech. |
| Score 1 | A response at this level is very short and practically not related to the task. It lacks substance beyond the expression of very basic ideas and is hard for the listener to understand due to consistent pronunciation, stress, and intonation problems and a severely limited control of grammar and vocabulary. |
| Score 0 | A response at this level is not relevant to the task or has no substance. |

## 2. Integrated Tasks (Tasks 2-4)

**Score 4**

A response at this level effectively addresses the task by presenting the necessary information and appropriate details. It generally shows clear, fluid, sustained speech and effective control of grammar and vocabulary. Though it may have minor errors in pronunciation, intonation, or language use, they do not affect the overall intelligibility or meaning.

**Score 3**

A response at this level addresses the task appropriately but is not fully developed. It conveys the necessary information but does not include sufficient details. It shows generally clear speech with some fluidity of expression, but minor problems with pronunciation, intonation, or pacing may result in some listener effort. It also displays somewhat effective use of grammar and vocabulary despite the existence of some incorrect word choice or language structures.

**Score 2**

A response at this level conveys some relevant information, but the ideas are not well connected. It omits key ideas, shows limited development, or exhibits a misunderstanding of key ideas. It shows clear speech occasionally but mostly demonstrates difficulties with pronunciation, intonation, or pace of speech—problems that require significant listener effort. It also displays only a basic level of grammar and vocabulary, which results in a limited or vague expression of ideas or unclear connections.

**Score 1**

A response at this level is very short and practically not related to the task. It fails to provide much relevant content and contains inaccurate or vague expressions of ideas. It is characterized by fragmented speech with frequent pauses and hesitations and consistent pronunciation and intonation problems. It also shows a severely limited range and control of grammar and vocabulary.

**Score 0**

A response at this level is not relevant to the task or has no substance.

# B-1

## Building Knowledge & Skills for the Speaking Test

# Task **1** | **Choosing a Career**

**Q** Some people say we should not rely on other people's advice when deciding on a career. Others say we should consider the advice of others. Which do you prefer?

---

◈ **Planning** Plan an answer for both options. Some ideas have been provided to help you.

▷ **Don't Rely on Advice**

Supporting Detail 1:

Supporting Detail 2:

> **Idea Box**
>
> Other people may not have the same goals in my life as I do.
> Only I can really know what type of work I would like to do.
> Another person's opinion might be good for that individual but not for me.

▷ **Rely on Advice**

Supporting Detail 1:

Supporting Detail 2:

> **Idea Box**
>
> Someone with more life experience can give me an educated opinion.
> There may be some career options I have not considered, and others can inform me of them.
> Other people can sometimes see things in us that we cannot see.

◈ **Speaking** Now give your spoken response for 45 seconds.

| Response time: 45 seconds | Your speaking time: _____ seconds |
|---|---|

**Transitions** *and* **Canned Phrases**

| If I rely on someone else's advice, then… | Not taking others' advice could… |
|---|---|
| Taking others' advice may also… | … might happen, too, if I don't listen to others. |

◈ **Comparing** Listen to a sample response and compare it with yours.

Don't Rely on Advice    Rely on Advice

02-01          02-02

# Task 2 | New Student Activities Fee

---

**Vocabulary** Take a few moments to review the vocabulary items that will appear in this task.

**fund** *v.* to provide money for

**commute** *v.* to travel back and forth, esp. by car

**stick around** *phr v.* to wait

**socialize** *v.* to enjoy one's free time with others

**tuition** *n.* a fee paid for education

**chip in** *phr v.* to contribute toward the cost of something

---

**Sample Response** | Prearrange your understanding of the task with the activities below.

The announcement states that the university's student activities fee will be increased from seventy-five to 100 dollars because of the economy. The fee funds various student activities and organizations, but it is not mandatory, and students can opt out of it. The man is upset about the increase and says there is no way he will pay it. The first reason for his opinion is that he reads the newspaper but does not make use of the other things the fee funds, such as student activities and athletic clubs. He also stresses that he cannot afford the increase by saying that the fee would require him to work more hours at his job. Even though the female student points out that fifty dollars is small compared to the annual tuition, the male student says that it would be five more hours of work for something that does not benefit him.

02-03

**Analyzing** Locate and underline the transition words and phrases used in the response.

**Deducing** Based on the information in the response, complete the following outline for the reading and the listening.

**Reading**
Topic:

**Listening**
Speaker's Opinion:

Reason 1:

Reason 2:

◈ **Reading** Read the following passage about a university's increased student activities fee.

Reading Time: 45 Seconds

## Increased Student Activities Fee

The Undergraduate Council of Students at City University has received approval to raise the yearly student activities fee to 125 dollars a year, up from seventy-five dollars, in response to the struggling economy. The fee funds the student newspaper, the amateur literary magazine, athletics clubs, the student recreation center, and annual student events such as the Spring Fling. The fee is optional; students may fill out a waiver at the Finance Office. However, students who opt out of the fee will not be permitted access to any of the student events. Please note the fee is covered by financial aid packages.

**(Checking)** Give a brief spoken response for each question.

**1** Why did the student council decide to raise the student activities fee?

**2** What do students receive for the fee?

**3** How should students respond if they don't want to pay the fee?

**4 Critical Thinking:** Why might some people choose not to pay the fee?

◈ **Listening** Listen to two students as they discuss the above information and take notes.

> **• Note •**
>
> **Speaker's Opinion:**
>
> 02-04
>
> Reason 1:
>
> Reason 2:

# Q
The man expresses his opinion about the increased fee. Explain his opinion and the reasons he gives for holding it.

---

◆ **Planning** Plan your response by using the information from the reading and the listening.

**His Opinion:**


Reason 1:


Reason 2:


### Transitions *and* Canned Phrases

The man feels that the fee is unfair because...          The man is upset about the increased fee...

One reason the man feels this way is...                  His first reason for his opinion is...

Second, the man thinks that...                           He also mentions that...


◆ **Speaking** Now give your spoken response for 60 seconds.

| Response time: 60 seconds | Your speaking time: _____ seconds |
| --- | --- |

## Task 3 | Anthropology: Early Civilizations

**Vocabulary** Take a few moments to review the vocabulary items that will appear in this task.

**densely populated** *exp.* having a high ratio of population to land

**unsanitary** *adj.* not clean or healthy

**slum** *n.* an area with high poverty and poor living conditions

**sewage** *n.* an area for carrying human waste

**surpass** *v.* to go beyond or above

**feat** *n.* an impressive accomplishment

**uniform** *adj.* being the same

**intricate** *adj.* with high attention to detail; exact

---

### Sample Response | Prearrange your understanding of the task with the activities below.

The reading states that human civilization arose after the rise of agriculture in 9500 B.C. and claims that the Indus Valley Civilization was remarkable for its technological advancements, especially in science and urban planning. The professor explains further by giving two examples of advanced technology in the Indus Valley Civilization. The professor begins by describing how urban planning was used in that civilization. He says that even though the people lived in densely populated urban areas, they were not unsanitary. The reason is that the cities had advanced pipe systems, which allowed sewage systems to be built and water to be piped into everyone's home. The professor also points out that the intricate measuring system allowed for perfect ratios in building bricks. These examples show that the Indus Valley Civilization had urban planning and measuring systems superior to any of that time period, which makes it remarkable and unique.

02-05

**Analyzing** Locate and underline the transition words and phrases used in the response.

**Deducing** Based on the information in the sample response, complete the following outline about the reading and the listening.

**Reading**
Topic:

**Listening**
Main Idea:

Supporting Detail 1:

Supporting Detail 2:

◈ **Reading** Read the following passage about early civilizations.

Reading Time: 45 Seconds

## Early Civilizations

With the innovation of agriculture around 9500 B.C., humans slowly shifted from nomadic hunter-gatherers to farmers living in various types of agrarian communities. For several thousand years, people lived in relatively small communities. It was not until the fourth millennium B.C. that civilizations—that is, unified communities exhibiting advanced arts, materials development, and record keeping—began to appear. Of the major early civilizations, the Indus Valley Civilization stands out as an intriguing place for archaeologists and anthropologists for its remarkable advancements in science and urban planning.

(**Checking**) Give a brief spoken response for each question.

1 Explain how people lived after the innovation of agriculture.

2 What is a civilization?

3 What is remarkable about the Indus Valley Civilization?

4 **Critical Thinking:** How are archaeology and anthropology useful to the progress of human society?

◈ **Listening** Listen to part of a lecture on the same topic and take notes.

┌─• **Note** •─────────────────────────────────┐
│                                              │
│                                    02-06     │
│                                              │
│                                              │
│                                              │
│                                              │
│                                              │
│                                              │
└──────────────────────────────────────────────┘

**Q** The professor explains how the people of the Indus Valley advanced science and urban planning. Explain how these examples demonstrate that the Indus Valley civilization was remarkable.

---

◈ **Planning** Plan your response by using the information from the reading and the listening.

**Main Idea:**



Supporting Detail 1:



Supporting Detail 2:




**Transitions *and* Canned Phrases**

The reading is about…                                    The professor starts by…
In the lecture, the professor states…                    The first example given by the professor is…
The second example mentioned in the lecture…             Finally, the professor says…



◈ **Speaking** Now give your spoken response for 60 seconds.

| Response time: 60 seconds | Your speaking time: _____ seconds |
|---|---|

# Task 4 | Economics: The Labor Theory of Value

**Vocabulary** Take a few moments to review the vocabulary items that will appear in this task.

**sneakers** *n.* tennis shoes; casual shoes

**mainstream** *adj.* widely accepted; popular

**neglect** *v.* to fail to do; to leave out

**foundational** *adj.* basic; essential

**primitive** *adj.* not advanced; at an early stage of development

**commodity** *n.* something bought and sold

## Sample Response | Prearrange your understanding of the task with the activities below.

The professor explains the labor theory of value by explaining the positions of Adam Smith and Karl Marx. Adam Smith stated that products' costs should be determined by how much labor was required to produce them, not by market forces. To illustrate this, the professor gives an example of cars and motorcycles. If cars take three times more work to produce than motorcycles do, then cars should be three times as expensive. However, Smith said that capitalism should take over after a society advances. In contrast, Karl Marx believed the labor theory of value should always take the place of capitalism. He argued that labor power is not paid fairly by capitalists. In other words, workers are exploited by capitalists. As an example, Marx said that if workers in a factory were paid a fair salary, then profits would be impossible. So while Smith and Marx disagreed on some details, they both believed in using labor to determine a product's value.

02-07

**Analyzing** Locate and underline the transition words and phrases used in the response.

**Deducing** Based on the information in the response, complete the following outline for the listening.

Topic:

Main Idea:

Supporting Detail 1:

Supporting Detail 2:

◈ **Listening** Listen to a short lecture and take notes.

┌─ • Note • ─────────────────────────────────────┐
│                                                 │
│                                        [QR code]│
│                                          02-08  │
│                                                 │
│                                                 │
│                                                 │
│                                                 │
└─────────────────────────────────────────────────┘

**Q** Using points and examples from the lecture, explain the labor theory of value.

---------------------------------------------------------------------------------------

◈ **Planning** Plan your response by using the information from the lecture.

**Main Idea:**


Supporting Detail 1:


Supporting Detail 2:


### Transitions *and* Canned Phrases

The professor discusses…                    He begins by talking about…
This point is made clear with the example of…    To explain, he gives an example about…
The second point in the lecture is about…    This theory is explained with…


◈ **Speaking** Now give your spoken response for 60 seconds.

| Response time: 60 seconds | Your speaking time: _____ seconds |
|---|---|

## Chapter 02

# Task **1** | Exms vs. Coursework

 Some people believe that examinations are the best way to assess students. Others say that coursework is better. Which do you think is better and why?

---

◆ **Planning** Plan an answer for both options. Some ideas have been provided to help you.

▷ **Examinations**

Supporting Detail 1:

Supporting Detail 2:

### ·ᶤ· Idea Box

There must be a reason why virtually all institutions use examinations: because they work.

If a student has learned everything he or she should have learned, then the student should pass an exam.

An examination is the only way teachers can assess each student's performance without bias.

▷ **Coursework**

Supporting Detail 1:

Supporting Detail 2:

### ·ᶤ· Idea Box

Not everybody is a good test taker.

Coursework makes up the majority of a student's class-related activities.

Coursework is usually more varied and allows students to demonstrate multiple skill sets.

◆ **Speaking** Now give your spoken response for 45 seconds.

| Response time: 45 seconds | Your speaking time: _____ seconds |
| --- | --- |

### Transitions *and* Canned Phrases

It is my belief that… is the best way to assess students.

First, examinations allow the teacher…

As an example, there was one time that I…

There are a couple of reasons for my opinion.

First, coursework is more… than exams.

To illustrate my point…

◆ **Comparing** Listen to a sample response and compare it with yours.

Examinations

Coursework

02-09
    02-10

## Task 2 | Emergency-Help Buttons

**Vocabulary** Take a few moments to review the vocabulary items that will appear in this task.

**kiosk** *n.* a small structure, often open on one or more sides

**patrol** *v.* to move around an area systematically, especially to protect or observe it

**measure** *n.* an action that is taken to achieve a goal

**relatively** *adv.* compared to other similar things

**paranoid** *adj.* overly nervous, worried, and anxious

**mug** *v.* to assault and rob

---

**Sample Response** | Prearrange your understanding of the task with the activities below.

The announcement is about some emergency kiosks that will be placed around the campus for the students' safety. Students can press the button at the kiosk and get help from campus police within two minutes. The woman is not in favor of the emergency kiosks. She begins by saying that the kiosks will reduce her comfort level on campus. The kiosks give her the impression that the campus isn't safe. She begins to wonder if the university is in a dangerous area, and she claims that the kiosks may make her become paranoid. She also feels that a two-minute response time is not fast enough during an actual emergency. The man compares this response time to response times off campus, but she insists that if she is being mugged or attacked, she won't have time to stand around for two minutes waiting on the police to arrive.

02-11

**Analyzing** Locate and underline the transition words and phrases used in the response.

**Deducing** Based on the information in the response, complete the following outline for the reading and the listening.

**Reading**

Topic:

**Listening**

Speaker's Opinion:

Reason 1:

Reason 2:

## ◈ Reading Read the following announcement about emergency-help kiosks.

Reading Time: 45 Seconds

### Emergency-Help Kiosks

In the coming weeks, the university will be installing some emergency-help kiosks all across campus. The metal kiosks will be situated all along campus sidewalks and outside of various buildings and can easily be located by a large red flag attached to a 10-foot pole. Students who feel in danger can press an emergency-help button at a kiosk, and campus police will immediately be notified. Nearby patrolling police will be alerted. Sergeant Davis of the campus police estimates that the response time should be no more than two minutes. The university hopes this measure will increase security on campus.

**(Checking)** Give a brief spoken response for each question.

1 What do the emergency-help kiosks look like?

2 Where will the kiosks be found?

3 How will the kiosks work to keep students safe?

4 **Critical Thinking:** How could the kiosks be improved to make them more effective?

## ◈ Listening Listen to two students as they discuss the above information and take notes.

┌─ **• Note •** ──────────────────────────────

**Speaker's Opinion:**

02-12

Reason 1:

Reason 2:

└──────────────────────────────────────

**Q** The woman expresses her opinion about the emergency-help kiosks. Explain her opinion and the reasons she gives for holding it.

◆ **Planning** Plan your response by using the information from the reading and the listening.

**Her Opinion:**

Reason 1:

Reason 2:

**Transitions *and* Canned Phrases**

| | |
|---|---|
| The announcement is about… | The woman feels that the kiosks… |
| First, she says that… | Her first reason is that the kiosks… |
| Second, the woman does not think… | She also believes that… |

◆ **Speaking** Now give your spoken response for 60 seconds.

| Response time: 60 seconds | Your speaking time: _____ seconds |
|---|---|

## Task 3 | Animal Science: Scavenging

---

**Vocabulary**   Take a few moments to review the vocabulary items that will appear in this task.

**carnivore**  *n.*  an animal that eats meat

**prey**  *n.*  an organism that is hunted for food

**predator**  *n.*  an organism that hunts other animals for food

**corpse**  *n.*  a dead body

**predilection**  *n.*  a natural tendency toward some behavior

**wounded**  *adj.*  hurt; injured

**heavy lifting**  *n.*  difficult or tiring work

**proactive**  *adj.*  acting in advance to avoid future difficulty

**devour**  *v.*  to eat quickly

**carcass**  *n.*  a dead body

---

**Sample Response** | Prearrange your understanding of the task with the activities below.

The reading introduces the concept of scavengers as animals that eat the corpses of prey that were killed by other predators. It also says that some scavengers hunt if necessary. The professor elaborates on the concept of scavenger animals by giving examples of scavengers that don't hunt and those that do. She begins with the vulture. The vulture, according the professor, circles overhead sick or dying animals and finishes them off if necessary, but it will not hunt down healthy prey like normal predators do. She then moves on to explain that some scavengers actually hunt down animals. The example she gives is the hyena. While hyenas prefer to wait for lions or other animals to kill animals and to have their fill, they are no strangers to the hunt. They hunt down and completely devour animals if there are no carcasses available for them to scavenge.

02-13

**Analyzing**   Locate and underline the transition words and phrases used in the response.

**Deducing**   Based on the information in the sample response, complete the following outline about the reading and the listening.

### Reading

Topic:

### Listening

Main Idea:

Supporting Detail 1:

Supporting Detail 2:

# ◈ Reading   Read the following passage about scavenging.

Reading Time: 45 Seconds

## Scavenging

   Among carnivores in the wild, most hunt prey animals for food. However, some animals practice scavenging, which is the consumption of an animal that has already been killed. These animals may have been killed by predators, by natural events, or by an outside force, such as being struck by a passing vehicle. While most scavengers tend to rely on finding corpses for food, there are a few species that, despite their predilection for scavenging, hunt if necessary.

**(Checking)** Give a brief spoken response for each question.

1 How are scavengers different from other carnivores?

2 What do scavengers rely on for food?

3 What are the different types of scavengers introduced in the reading passage?

4 **Critical Thinking:** Why might some scavengers be more likely to hunt than others?

# ◈ Listening   Listen to part of a lecture on the same topic and take notes.

**• Note •**

02-14

**Q** The professor describes scavengers by providing two examples. Explain how these examples demonstrate what scavengers are and how they may differ from one another.

---------------------------------------------------------------------------------------------

◆ **Planning** Plan your response by using the information from the reading and the listening.

**Main Idea:**


Supporting Detail 1:


Supporting Detail 2:


**Transitions** *and* **Canned Phrases**

The reading introduces the concept of…          The main difference between… and… is…
The professor begins by describing…             This is explained further with…
Next, the professor mentions…                   She also explains that…

◆ **Speaking** Now give your spoken response for 60 seconds.

| | |
|---|---|
| Response time: 60 seconds | Your speaking time: _____ seconds |

## Task 4 | Astronomy: Ultra-Massive Stars

**Vocabulary** Take a few moments to review the vocabulary items that will appear in this task.

**solar mass** *n.* a unit of measurement equal to the mass of the sun

**undergo** *v.* to endure; to experience

**collapse** *v.* to fall inward because of a loss of support

**core** *n.* the center

**atmospheric** *adj.* relating to the outer layers of a sphere

**dramatically** *v.* extremely; greatly

**remnant** *n.* a part that is left over; a remainder

**gravitational pull** *n.* the effect of gravity

**density** *n.* mass per unit measure

**velocity** *n.* the speed and direction of an object

### Sample Response | Prearrange your understanding of the task with the activities below.

The professor describes what happens when an ultra-massive star dies. Ultra-massive stars, which have a solar mass of at least 1.4, first go through a supernova phase. This begins when their outer shells very quickly collapse upon their cores because they have run out of energy. The resulting explosion sends atmospheric material flying through space. As this happens, the explosion creates an extremely bright light, which can sometimes be brighter than any other star in its galaxy. Next, depending on its mass, the star can do one of two things. If the star's solar mass is under five, then it becomes a neutron star. Neutron stars have a very high escape velocity that is one-third the speed of light. If the collapsed star's solar mass is over five, then it becomes a black hole, which has no escape velocity because of its extreme gravitational pull and density.

02-15

**Analyzing** Locate and underline the transition words and phrases used in the response.

**Deducing** Based on the information in the response, complete the following outline for the listening.

Topic:

Main Idea:

Supporting Detail 1:

Supporting Detail 2:

• Note •

02-16

**Q** Using points and examples from the lecture, explain what happens when ultra-massive stars die.

◈ **Planning** Plan your response by using the information from the lecture.

**Main Idea:**

Supporting Detail 1:

Supporting Detail 2:

**Transitions** *and* **Canned Phrases**

The topic of the lecture is…                    The first thing that happens…
When this happens, it causes…               Depending on the star's solar mass…
If… then…                                        Finally, an ultra-massive star may… if…

◈ **Speaking** Now give your spoken response for 60 seconds.

| Response time: 60 seconds | Your speaking time: _____ seconds |
|---|---|

## Task 1 | Career: Money or Enjoyment

**Q** Do you think it is better to have a job that you do not like but which earns a high salary or a job that you enjoy but which earns a low salary? Which do you prefer and why?

◆ **Planning** Plan an answer for both options. Some ideas have been provided to help you.

▷ **Salary 〉 Enjoyment**

Supporting Detail 1:

Supporting Detail 2:

**🔆 Idea Box**

A higher salary may enable one to have more enjoyable free time.

Some people find satisfaction in their income level and gain great enjoyment from that.

Earning a high salary may allow one to worry less about medical bills and retirement.

▷ **Enjoyment 〉 Salary**

Supporting Detail 1:

Supporting Detail 2:

**🔆 Idea Box**

People spend a great portion of their lives—usually 40 hours a week or more—at work.

When you die, you cannot take your money with you.

Many people develop their personalities around their chosen career.

◆ **Speaking** Now give your spoken response for 45 seconds.

| Response time: 45 seconds | Your speaking time: _____ seconds |

**Transitions** *and* **Canned Phrases**

I believe it is better to have a job that…

The most important goal in my life is…

The other reason is that…

I'd prefer to have a job that…

Having a job that… would allow me to…

If I have a job that… then…

◆ **Comparing** Listen to a sample response and compare it with yours.

Salary 〉 Enjoyment   Enjoyment 〉 Salary

02-17

02-18

# Task 2 | Road Closure

---

**Vocabulary** Take a few moments to review the vocabulary items that will appear in this task.

**traffic** *n.* all the vehicles that are on a road

**pedestrian** *n.* a person who is walking, often alongside a road

**destination** *n.* the place where a person is going

**detour** *n.* an alternate route that often must be taken since a regular route is closed

**inconvenience** *n.* the act of not suiting a person's needs or purposes

**group punishment** *n.* the act of penalizing everyone in a group

---

## Sample Response | Prearrange your understanding of the task with the activities below.

The man and the woman are having a conversation about the school's decision to close Martinson Road to all vehicular traffic. From now on, only pedestrians will be allowed on the road. The reason given for this change is that there have been too many accidents involving vehicles and pedestrians on the road. The woman has mixed feelings about the decision by the university. On the one hand, she understands the decision because too many people have gotten hurt lately. She states that there have been five accidents on the road in just one month. One of the people who was injured in an accident there is her friend, who is still in the hospital. On the other hand, she comments that she dislikes group punishment. She explains that every driver is being punished by the actions of a few irresponsible drivers. In that regard, she dislikes the way that the school is handling the situation.

02-19

**Analyzing** Locate and underline the transition words and phrases used in the response.

**Deducing** Based on the information in the response, complete the following outline for the reading and the listening.

**Reading**

Topic:

**Listening**

Speaker's Opinion:

Reason 1:

Reason 2:

◆**Reading**  Read the following passage about a road closure on a university campus.

Reading Time: 45 Seconds

## Martinson Road to Be Closed to Traffic

Martinson Road, which runs through the middle of the campus, will now be closed to all traffic. This includes cars, trucks, vans, motorbikes, and even bicycles. Only individuals who are walking will be permitted on Martinson Road as of Monday, February 11. Recently, there have been several accidents involving vehicles and pedestrians on the road. We at City University take the safety of our students carefully, so we have decided to close the road to vehicles. This will enable students safely to walk to their classes and other destinations. For more information, please speak with the campus police.

(**Checking**)  Give a brief spoken response for each question.

**1** What is City University changing about Martinson Road?

**2** Why has City University decided to make the change?

**3** What does City University hope will be the result of this change?

**4 Critical Thinking:** What are some other ways to make a university campus safe for pedestrians?

◆**Listening**  Listen to two students as they discuss the above information and take notes.

---• **Note** •----

**Speaker's Opinion:**

02-20

Reason 1:

Reason 2:

**Q** The woman expresses her opinion about a road closure. Explain her opinion and the reasons she gives for holding it.

------------------------------------------------------------------------------------------

◆ **Planning** Plan your response by using the information from the reading and the listening.

**Her Opinion:**


Reason 1:



Reason 2:



**Transitions** *and* **Canned Phrases**

| | |
|---|---|
| The man and the woman are having a conversation about… | From now on… |
| The reason given for this change is… | On the one hand, she understands… |
| Yet on the other hand, she comments that… | In that regard, she… |


◆ **Speaking** Now give your spoken response for 60 seconds.

| Response time: 60 seconds | Your speaking time: _____ seconds |
|---|---|

# Task 3 | Natural Science: Bioluminescence

---

**Vocabulary** Take a few moments to review the vocabulary items that will appear in this task.

**byproduct** *n.* something produced while making another thing

**spectrum** *n.* a distribution of similar or related values

**glow** *n.* a soft light

**camouflage** *n.* a pattern or colors that make something hard to see

**appendage** *n.* a body part that sticks out from the body

**crustacean** *n.* a small, aquatic organism with an outer shell

**emit** *v.* to send out from a central location

**repel** *v.* to push away; to cause to avoid

**larva** *n.* the early wormlike stage of an insect's life cycle

**toxic** *adj.* poisonous

---

**Sample Response** | Prearrange your understanding of the task with the activities below.

Bioluminescence is the ability of plants and animals to produce light naturally. The light is used for a number of different reasons. The professor begins by giving examples of sea creatures that produce light in the deep sea. The first that he mentions is the anglerfish, which has an appendage coming out from its head which the fish uses to attract prey. The professor also mentions crustaceans, which use light to attract potential mates.

02-21

The professor then moves on to give examples of land-dwelling organisms that produce light. The first example of fireflies illustrates again the ability of creatures to use bioluminescence to attract mates. In addition to fireflies, there are also glowing mushrooms in the forest. Their light is possibly used to signal to predators that the mushrooms are toxic, but scientists are unsure of exactly what purpose the light serves.

**Analyzing** Locate and underline the transition words and phrases used in the response.

**Deducing** Based on the information in the sample response, complete the following outline about the reading and the listening.

### Reading

Topic:

### Listening

Main Idea:

Supporting Detail 1:

Supporting Detail 2:

◆ **Reading** Read the following passage about bioluminescence.

Reading Time: 45 Seconds

## Bioluminescence

Because of natural conditions of extreme darkness, certain organisms have evolved the ability to produce light naturally. This ability, known as bioluminescence, is a byproduct of chemical reactions either inside or outside of the cells of organisms. The resulting light usually belongs in the blue and green spectrum although a few species produce a dark red or yellow glow. The light is useful to species in a number of different ways. Its most frequent use is for the attraction of mates or prey or for camouflage although scientists speculate it may also be used for communication or for the repulsion of potential predators.

**(Checking)** Give a brief spoken response for each question.

**1** What is bioluminescence?

**2** What color is the light produced via bioluminescence?

**3** How do animals and other organisms make use of bioluminescence?

**4 Critical Thinking:** In what other ways might organisms evolve to adapt to extremely dark environments?

◆ **Listening** Listen to part of a lecture on the same topic and take notes.

┌─ **Note** ─────────────────────────────────┐

02-22

└─────────────────────────────────────────┘

**Q** The professor describes bioluminescence by giving examples of where and how it is used. Explain how these examples demonstrate the function and the purpose of bioluminescence.

◈ **Planning** Plan your response by using the information from the reading and the listening.

**Main Idea:**


Supporting Detail 1:


Supporting Detail 2:


**Transitions** *and* **Canned Phrases**

According to the reading, bioluminescence is…          Bioluminescence is used to…

The professor begins by explaining…          Deep-sea creatures use bioluminescence to…

Some forest creatures also exhibit…          This is used by… to…


◈ **Speaking** Now give your spoken response for 60 seconds.

| Response time: 60 seconds | Your speaking time: _____ seconds |
|---|---|

# Task 4 | Sociology: Social Construction

**Vocabulary**  Take a few moments to review the vocabulary items that will appear in this task.

**perceive**  *v.*  to understand; to analyze sense data

**jammed**  *adj.*  stuck in place; unable to be moved easily

**ram**  *v.*  to hit with great force, especially in order to move

**burglary**  *n.*  the act of robbing a home or business

**sergeant**  *n.*  an organizational rank

**arrest**  *v.*  to take into police custody

**procedure**  *n.*  a way of doing something

**facet**  *n.*  an aspect of something

**interpret**  *v.*  to understand based on personal knowledge

**genuine**  *adj.*  real; authentic

## Sample Response | Prearrange your understanding of the task with the activities below.

The professor uses an anecdote to explain the concept of social construction, which means that we each have a subjective perception of reality. The professor begins the lecture with a story which is about an African-American Harvard professor who is arrested at his own home. The police officer in the story is Caucasian, and he arrests the professor, who appeared to have been breaking into his own home. The two men in the story interpreted the event very differently—one as a racist act and the other as a simple police procedure. The professor then explains that this story illustrates social construction. This is the idea that no person has a true objective perception of reality and that instead we each understand the world based on our own experiences and knowledge. As illustrated in the example of the Harvard professor and the police officer, social construction can create problems in our everyday lives due to misunderstandings.

02-23

**Analyzing**  Locate and underline the transition words and phrases used in the response.

**Deducing**  Based on the information in the response, complete the following outline for the listening.

Topic:

Main Idea:

Supporting Detail 1:

Supporting Detail 2:

◈ **Listening** Listen to a short lecture and take notes.

┌─ • **Note** • ─────────────────────────────────────────────┐
│                                                              │
│                                              [QR code]       │
│                                               02-24          │
│                                                              │
│                                                              │
│                                                              │
│                                                              │
└──────────────────────────────────────────────────────────────┘

**Q** Using points and examples from the lecture, explain the concept of social construction.

---

◈ **Planning** Plan your response by using the information from the lecture.

**Main Idea:**


Supporting Detail 1:


Supporting Detail 2:


┌─────────────────────────────┐
│ **Transitions** *and* **Canned Phrases** │
└─────────────────────────────┘

The lecture begins with a story about...          The story involves...
The professor uses the story to explain...        Social construction, in a nutshell, is...
Social construction affects our lives by...        The lecture concludes with...


◈ **Speaking** Now give your spoken response for 60 seconds.

┌──────────────────────────────────────────────────────────────┐
│        Response time: 60 seconds        Your speaking time: _____ seconds │
└──────────────────────────────────────────────────────────────┘

# Task 1 | Teaching Formally vs. Teaching Casually

 **Q** Some students prefer instructors who teach formally while other students prefer instructors who teach casually. Talk about the advantages and disadvantages of teaching formally [casually]. Use details and examples to explain your answers.

◊ **Planning** Plan an answer for both options. Some ideas have been provided to help you.

▷ **Teach Formally**

Advantages:

Disadvantages:

### ☀ Idea Box

Formal instructors are better able to control their students during class.
Students often listen better in formal classes, so they learn more.
Formal instructors usually just give lectures rather than allow class discussions.

▷ **Teach Casually**

Advantages:

Disadvantages:

### ☀ Idea Box

Casual instructors are more fun than instructors who teach formally.
More students are willing to talk in class discussions led by casual instructors.
Some students do not show much respect when instructors behave casually.

◊ **Speaking** Now give your spoken response for 45 seconds.

| Response time: 45 seconds | Your speaking time: _____ seconds |
|---|---|

### Transitions *and* Canned Phrases

First of all, formal instructors often…
The reason is that they…
Casual instructors have a tendency to…

Students also tend to…
First of all, one advantage is that…
On the negative side, students…

◊ **Comparing** Listen to a sample response and compare it with yours.

Teach Formally

Teach Casually

02-25

02-26

## Task 2 | New Internet-Based Courses

**Vocabulary** Take a few moments to review the vocabulary items that will appear in this task.

**virtual** *adj.* performed online rather than in person

**conduct** *v.* to direct, manage, or control

**commute** *v.* to travel back and forth, especially for work or school

**brick and mortar** *exp.* done in a building rather than online

**outdated** *adj.* old-fashioned

**banter** *n.* a lively discussion

**elicit** *v.* to draw out; to call forth

**procrastinate** *v.* needlessly to delay necessary work

**Sample Response** | Prearrange your understanding of the task with the activities below.

The students are discussing an announcement about new online courses being offered at the university. At first, the woman is interested in the online courses, but after some discussion, she decides that she is not a good candidate for them. Her first reason for her opinion is that she feels she is a brick-and-mortar type of person. This means that she enjoys being in a physical location to take a class more than she would enjoy studying online. The man says the Internet is the way of the future, but she says that she likes to discuss topics with other students and the professor in the classroom so that she can better understand the material. She also states that she doesn't think she is self-motivated enough to complete an online course. She worries that she will procrastinate and not get her coursework completed on time.

02-27

**Analyzing** Locate and underline the transition words and phrases used in the response.

**Deducing** Based on the information in the response, complete the following outline for the reading and the listening.

**Reading**

Topic:

**Listening**

Speaker's Opinion:

Reason 1:

Reason 2:

◈ **Reading** Read the following passage about Internet-based courses.

Reading Time: 45 Seconds

## Internet-Based Courses

City University is proud to announce the availability of a selection of Internet-based courses beginning the next academic year. The courses will be available through the university network system on secure servers. Students who participate in the online courses will need to purchase the required reading material but will not be required to physically attend lectures. However, some professors may require their students to attend virtual lectures conducted via webcam. Students who wish to sign up for online classes may contact their academic advisor. Please note that commuting students have priority in the case of high-demand courses.

( **Checking** ) Give a brief spoken response for each question.

**1** What is the new course program being offered by City University?

**2** How do students participate in the program?

**3** What will students need to do if they wish to sign up for the program?

**4 Critical Thinking:** Why would the university give priority to commuting students?

◈ **Listening** Listen to two students as they discuss the above information and take notes.

┌─ • **Note** • ─────────────────────────────────┐

**Speaker's Opinion:**

02-28

Reason 1:

Reason 2:

└──────────────────────────────────────────────┘

# Q

The woman expresses her opinion about the new online courses. State her opinion and the reasons she gives for holding it.

◆ **Planning** Plan your response by using the information from the reading and the listening.

**Her Opinion:**

Reason 1:

Reason 2:

**Transitions** *and* **Canned Phrases**

The woman thinks online courses are (not) for her because...

Her first reason is that...
She also feels that...

◆ **Speaking** Now give your spoken response for 60 seconds.

| Response time: 60 seconds | Your speaking time: _____ seconds |

## Task 3 │ Philosophy: Transcendentalism

---

**⊢ Vocabulary** Take a few moments to review the vocabulary items that will appear in this task. ⊢

**rational** *adj.* using logic and reason

**contemporary** *adj.* happening at the same time

**precursor** *n.* something that comes before another thing

**denomination** *n.* a sub-grouping within a larger religious group

**orthodox** *adj.* strictly following traditional rules and beliefs

**sect** *n.* a small group that differs from the majority

**doctrine** *n.* the beliefs accepted by a religious group

**divine** *n.* a term referring to the Judeo-Christian God

---

**Sample Response** │ Prearrange your understanding of the task with the activities below.

The Transcendentalists were thinkers in the early nineteenth century who opposed the popular thought of their day and developed a philosophy from their discontent. At that time in New England, the dominant religious group was the Unitarians. They did not believe in strictly following church doctrine or biblical interpretations. Instead, they believed that people should use rational thought in order to understand the divine. In contrast, the Transcendentalists felt that the divine was everywhere around them and was one and the same with nature. They said that people cannot understand the divine without feeling nature. Thus, they opposed the "corpse cold" Unitarian group and began their new philosophy, which emphasized learning to appreciate nature as a way to see God. So Transcendentalism came not only from a love of nature and the desire to see the divine through it but also from a resistance to contemporary religious philosophy.

02-29

**Analyzing** Locate and underline the transition words and phrases used in the response.

**Deducing** Based on the information in the sample response, complete the following outline about the reading and the listening.

### Reading
Topic:

### Listening
Main Idea:

Supporting Detail 1:

Supporting Detail 2:

◆ **Reading** Read the following passage about the Transcendentalist movement.

Reading Time: 45 Seconds

## The Transcendentalist Movement

In the early nineteenth century, a group of writers and thinkers in New England began delivering speeches and writing essays about a new religious philosophy. This group, which came to be known as the Transcendentalists, emphasized using one's senses rather than relying on a rational analysis of religious texts to learn spiritual truths. The movement laid out very few specific principles and thus cannot truly be understood outside of the religious context from which it sprang. Indeed, Transcendentalism was as much a rejection of contemporary modes of thought as a unique philosophy.

**Checking** Give a brief spoken response for each question.

**1** What was the goal of the Transcendentalist Movement?

**2** How did the Transcendentalists differ from other thinkers of their day?

**3** Why are the core principles of Transcendentalism difficult to understand?

**4 Critical Thinking:** What can be inferred about the people who began the Transcendentalist Movement?

◆ **Listening** Listen to part of a lecture on the same topic and take notes.

┌─ • **Note** • ─────────────────────────────────────────┐
│                                                          │
│                                              02-30       │
│                                                          │
│                                                          │
│                                                          │
│                                                          │
│                                                          │
│                                                          │
│                                                          │
│                                                          │
└──────────────────────────────────────────────────────────┘

**Q** The professor defines the Transcendentalist Movement by describing the era it arose from and how it differed from contemporary philosophy. Using information from the reading and the lecture, explain the origins of Transcendentalism and its unique philosophy.

---

◈ **Planning** Plan your response by using the information from the reading and the listening.

**Main Idea:**


Supporting Detail 1:


Supporting Detail 2:


### Transitions *and* Canned Phrases

The reading states that…

The Transcendentalists came about at a time when…

The professor supports the reading by saying…

According to the lecture, the Unitarians…

Instead, they believed that…


◈ **Speaking** Now give your spoken response for 60 seconds.

| Response time: 60 seconds | Your speaking time: _____ seconds |
|---|---|

## Task 4 | Business: Job Sharing

---

**Vocabulary** Take a few moments to review the vocabulary items that will appear in this task.

**reduced** *adj.* decreased; smaller in size, number, amount, etc.

**split** *v.* to divide into two or more parts

**appeal** *n.* the ability to interest or attract others

**arrangement** *n.* an agreement

**approach** *n.* a way or method of doing something

**strict** *adj.* the act of paying back money

**error** *n.* a mistake

**proliferate** *v.* to flourish; to increase in size, number, or amount

**colleague** *n.* a coworker; a person that one works with

**key** *adj.* important; major

---

**Sample Response** | Prearrange your understanding of the task with the activities below.

The professor lectures on job sharing. She defines it as a situation in which two or more people do the work that one person would normally do. She remarks that job sharers split the hours and the salary for their position. Job sharing is something parents with children like since they want to work yet also be with their children. The professor discusses two disadvantages of job sharing. The first is that job sharers may have different approaches to their jobs. She uses the example of two elementary school teachers splitting teaching duties. If one is strict while the other is not, then the students might become confused and not learn well. The second disadvantage she mentions is that there are often lots of communication errors. Colleagues need to keep the job sharers updated, but they might forget to do that at times. As a result, mistakes such as missed meetings or work that doesn't get done could happen.

02-31

**Analyzing** Locate and underline the transition words and phrases used in the response.

**Deducing** Based on the information in the response, complete the following outline for the listening.

Topic:

Main Idea:

Supporting Detail 1:

Supporting Detail 2:

◆ **Listening** Listen to a short lecture and take notes.

┌─ • Note • ─────────────────────────────────────────────────┐
│                                                    [QR code]  │
│                                                     02-32     │
│                                                              │
│                                                              │
│                                                              │
│                                                              │
│                                                              │
│                                                              │
└──────────────────────────────────────────────────────────────┘


**Q** Using points and examples from the lecture, explain what job sharing is and what some of its disadvantages are.

------------------------------------------------------------------------

◆ **Planning** Plan your response by using the information from the lecture.

**Main Idea:**


Supporting Detail 1:


Supportign Detail 2:



**Transitions *and* Canned Phrases**

The professor lectures on…                    The second disadvantage she mentions is that…
The professor discusses two advantages of…    As a result…
The first is that…


◆ **Speaking** Now give your spoken response for 60 seconds.

┌──────────────────────────────────────────────────────────────┐
│        Response time: 60 seconds     Your speaking time: _____ seconds │
└──────────────────────────────────────────────────────────────┘

## Chapter 05

# Task 1 | Living Alone vs. Roommates

 Some students prefer to live alone while at university. Other students prefer to have roommates. Please explain which you think is the better living situation.

---

◆ **Planning** Plan an answer for both options. Some ideas have been provided to help you.

▷ **Live Alone**

Supporting Detail 1:

Supporting Detail 2:

### :ϙ: Idea Box

Living alone might provide a quieter and more relaxing study environment.
Many people with roommates fight over messy habits or eating each other's food.
Without a roommate, you would have more privacy.

▷ **Have Roommates**

Supporting Detail 1:

Supporting Detail 2:

### :ϙ: Idea Box

It can get lonely living alone, especially if you don't have money to go out often.
Having roommates could help one adjust to a new environment, especially in a new city or country.
Sharing a room can help you develop important interpersonal skills.

◆ **Speaking** Now give your spoken response for 45 seconds.

| Response time: 45 seconds | Your speaking time: _____ seconds |
|---|---|

### Transitions *and* Canned Phrases

The best thing for me would be to...
If I had to live alone/with roommates...
I'd also prefer to have roommates because...

It goes without saying that...
Living alone would allow me to...
The most important thing is that...

◆ **Comparing** Listen to a sample response and compare it with yours.

Live Alone        Have Roommates

02-33            02-34

# Task 2 | Library Renovations

**Vocabulary** Take a few moments to review the vocabulary items that will appear in this task.

**renovation** *n.* rebuilding or redecorating to improve a building

**underway** *adj.* in the process of; having already begun

**foster** *v.* to promote; to facilitate

**approximate** *v.* to guess; to estimate

**reference** *n.* books used as sources of information

**as slow as molasses** *exp.* very slow

**database** *n.* a collection of computer-based data

**waiting list** *n.* a list that organizes shared resources or space

## Sample Response | Prearrange your understanding of the task with the activities below.

The two students are talking about the library being closed for renovations. The man is excited about the announcement because the renovations will improve the library in a couple of ways that will benefit him. The first thing that he mentions is that the computer lab will be improved. He says that he does not have a computer at home, so he does most of his computer-based research from on-campus computer labs. After the renovations, the computers in the library will access the database more quickly and facilitate his research. He also says that he is happy about the increased number of study rooms that will be added. Students currently must put their names on waiting lists in order to access study rooms. The man expects that, after the renovations, there will be plenty of rooms available, so waiting lists won't be needed.

02-35

**Analyzing** Locate and underline the transition words and phrases used in the response.

**Deducing** Based on the information in the response, complete the following outline for the reading and the listening.

**Reading**

Topic:

**Listening**

Speaker's Opinion:

Reason 1:

Reason 2:

◆ **Reading** Read the following passage about library renovations on a university campus.

Reading Time: 45 Seconds

## Library Renovations

The Robert F. Jenkins Library is pleased to announce that the renovation plans have passed final approval and remodeling will soon be underway. The library staff believes the changes will benefit the student body and foster academic achievement. Specific changes include an upgraded and expanded computer lab, updated versions of all key reference material, more group study rooms, and an overall redecoration of the library to make a more comfortable study environment for students. We approximate that the renovations, beginning in June, will take three to four months to complete. During that time, only reference material will be available.

**( Checking )** Give a brief spoken response for each question.

**1** What is the purpose of the announcement?

**2** In which ways will the library be improved due to the renovations?

**3** How will students be affected during the renovations?

**4 Critical Thinking:** Why might a student be upset about the changes?

◆ **Listening** Listen to two students as they discuss the above information and take notes.

--- • **Note** • ---

**Speaker's Opinion:**

02-36

Reason 1:

Reason 2:

# Q

The man expresses his opinion about the library renovations. Explain his opinion and the reasons he gives for holding it.

---

◆ **Planning** Plan your response by using the information from the reading and the listening.

**His Opinion:**

Reason 1:

Reason 2:

### Transitions *and* Canned Phrases

The man is happy about the changes because…

He mostly feels this way because…

He says that the renovations will…

Besides that, he thinks…

The man also says that…

In other words, he feels the renovations will…

◆ **Speaking** Now give your spoken response for 60 seconds.

| Response time: 60 seconds | Your speaking time: _____ seconds |
|---|---|

# Task 3 | Medicine: Penicillin

**Vocabulary** Take a few moments to review the vocabulary items that will appear in this task.

**mold** *n.* a growth of fungus

**culture** *n.* living matter grown for scientific study

**infectious** *adj.* able to be spread to others

**antibiotic** *n.* medicine used to stop infectious diseases

**revolutionize** *v.* to change in a drastic way

**viable** *adj.* able to continue successfully; sustainable

**cripple** *v.* to damage or weaken

**profound** *adj.* deep; far-reaching

**mortality** *n.* the quality of being able to die

**succumb** *v.* to give in to; to submit to a greater power

## Sample Response | Prearrange your understanding of the task with the activities below.

Penicillin was accidentally discovered by Alexander Fleming when he saw mold growing in a Petri dish he had left uncovered. The mold stopped infectious bacteria from spreading. This, the reading claims, changed the world. This argument is supported by the lecture. The professor begins the lecture by arguing that the advent of widespread penicillin use was the most important medical advancement in history. He says that before penicillin came into popular use, people usually became crippled or died from most infections. Penicillin also led the way to antibiotics becoming commonplace, which further improved public health. Another global impact of penicillin is on world population. The professor explains that the world's population would be about half of what it is today if not for penicillin. The reason is that many of our grandparents would have died from infections as children or as a result of wounds received in battle during wars.

02-37

**Analyzing** Locate and underline the transition words and phrases used in the response.

**Deducing** Based on the information in the sample response, complete the following outline about the reading and the listening.

**Reading**
Topic:

**Listening**
Main Idea:

Supporting Detail 1:

Supporting Detail 2:

◆ **Reading** Read the following passage about the discovery of penicillin.

Reading Time: 45 Seconds

## The Discovery of Penicillin

In 1928, Scottish scientist Alexander Fleming returned to his laboratory one morning to find a Petri dish he had accidentally left open had begun to grow mold. The Petri dish contained a culture of infectious bacteria Fleming had been studying. Curiously, the mold in the dish was surrounded by a ring through which the bacteria could not break through. Fleming grew a pure sample of the mold and learned that it could be used to fight off bacterial growth. He named his discovery— the world's first antibiotic—penicillin. Since that time, penicillin has revolutionized medicine and changed the world.

**Checking** Give a brief spoken response for each question.

**1** What did Alexander Fleming do that led to his discovery of penicillin?

**2** How was the mold found growing in the Petri dish unusual?

**3** What happened as a result of the discovery of penicillin?

**4 Critical Thinking:** How do you think the world would be different without penicillin?

◆ **Listening** Listen to part of a lecture on the same topic and take notes.

• **Note** •

02-38

**Q** The professor explains why penicillin is important to the world. Using points and examples from the lecture, explain what penicillin is and how it has benefitted the world.

---

◆ **Planning** Plan your response by using the information from the reading and the listening.

**Main Idea:**

Supporting Detail 1:

Supporting Detail 2:

**Transitions** *and* **Canned Phrases**

According to the reading, penicillin is…          Penicillin led the way to…
The professor claims that penicillin…            He mentions that in the past…
He furthers his argument by saying that…         Without penicillin…

◆ **Speaking** Now give your spoken response for 60 seconds.

| Response time: 60 seconds | Your speaking time: _____ seconds |
| --- | --- |

## Task 4 | Engineering: Arches

**Vocabulary** Take a few moments to review the vocabulary items that will appear in this task.

**innovation** *n.* something newly introduced

**arch** *n.* a curved structure that supports weight

**mobilization** *n.* sending out people in preparation for action

**sturdy** *adj.* well supported; unlikely to collapse or break

**adjacent** *adj.* directly next to

**mend** *v.* to fix; to make repairs

**ensure** *v.* to guarantee; to make certain

**loyalty** *n.* a feeling of strong support for

**conquer** *v.* to take control by force

**aqueduct** *n.* an aboveground structure that carries water

**Sample Response** | Prearrange your understanding of the task with the activities below.

According to the professor, innovations in engineering can alter the course of history. He makes this point by talking about how the Romans used arches to expand their empire. One of the ways they used arches was in the construction of bridges. Since the Roman Empire was spread all across Europe, there was very much terrain that needed to be crossed by the army. The arch allowed the Romans to create sturdy bridges, which in turn allowed the army to quickly travel to any location in Europe that needed immediate military attention. The other way the Romans spread their empire by using arches was with aqueducts. Arches allowed the construction of aqueducts to carry water to conquered people. Because providing water to ordinary people was unheard of at the time, the people became loyal to the Roman Empire. So by providing quick mobilization and gaining people's loyalty, arches helped the spread of the Roman Empire.

02-39

**Analyzing** Locate and underline the transition words and phrases used in the response.

**Deducing** Based on the information in the response, complete the following outline for the listening.

Topic:

Main Idea:

Supporting Detail 1:

Supporting Detail 2:

◊ **Listening** Listen to a short lecture and take notes.

┌─ • **Note** • ──────────────────────────────────────────┐
│                                                          │
│                                              [QR code]   │
│                                              02-40        │
│                                                          │
│                                                          │
│                                                          │
│                                                          │
│                                                          │
└──────────────────────────────────────────────────────────┘

**Q** Using points and examples from the lecture, explain how the Romans used arches to spread their empire across Europe.

------------------------------------------------------------------------------------

◊ **Planning** Plan your response by using the information from the lecture.

**Main Idea:**


Supporting Detail 1:


Supporting Detail 2:


**Transitions** *and* **Canned Phrases**

The main idea of the lecture is…                Rome was the first to…
The Romans used arches to…                      The first example the professor gives is…
This helped spread the Roman Empire by…         It also promoted the empire by…


◊ **Speaking** Now give your spoken response for 60 seconds.

| Response time: 60 seconds | Your speaking time: _____ seconds |

# B-1

## Chapter 06

**Independent Speaking**

# Task 1 | How to Use a New Piece of Equipment

 **Q** You are going to use a piece of equipment for the first time. Which of the following would you prefer to do?

✦ *Consult the user's manual*

✦ *Ask another person for assistance*

✦ *Watch an instructional video online*

Include specific details and reasons in your response.

---

◈ **Planning** Plan an answer for two options. Some ideas have been provided to help you.

▷ **Consult the User's Manual**

Supporting Detail 1:

Supporting Detail 2:

### ☼ Idea Box

You can find out exactly what to do with the user's manual.

You can learn about common mistakes people make.

You will learn how to avoid dangerous problems.

▷ **Ask Another Person for Assistance**

Supporting Detail 1:

Supporting Detail 2:

### ☼ Idea Box

You can learn from someone with experience using the equipment.

You can find out important information not in the user's manual.

You can get some tips on how to use the equipment more efficiently.

◈ **Speaking** Now give your spoken response for 45 seconds.

| Response time: 45 seconds | Your speaking time: _____ seconds |
|---|---|

### Transitions *and* Canned Phrases

| | |
|---|---|
| Of the three choices, I would opt to… | The primary reason is that… |
| Because they did that, they… | He explained precisely how to… |
| If I hadn't…, I might have… | A secondary reason is that… |

◈ **Comparing** Listen to a sample response and compare it with yours.

Consult the    Ask Another Person
User's Manual    for Assistance

02-41      02-42

# Task 2 | New Dormitory Opening

**Vocabulary** Take a few moments to review the vocabulary items that will appear in this task.

**sq. ft. – square foot** *n.* a measurement equal to one foot by one foot

**kitchenette** *n.* a small kitchen

**rip-off** *n.* something that is highly overpriced

**grocery** *n.* food, especially bought to supply a home

**curfew** *n.* the latest time by which a person must be home

**miss out** *phr v.* not to take an opportunity or experience

## Sample Response | Prearrange your understanding of the task with the activities below.

The woman sees the announcement about the new, high-quality dormitory on campus but decides that she does not want to live there. Her first reason for having that opinion is that she thinks the dorm is too expensive. At 14,000 dollars a year, it is almost 6,000 dollars more expensive than the other dorms. Instead, she prefers to find an apartment off campus, which she thinks will cost much less overall, even after she considers the cost of rent and groceries. She also says that she does not wish to follow the rules of the dormitory. Even though she would like to be on campus to participate in activities and to involve herself in the community, she does not think she can abide by the restrictions placed on students in dorms. One of the rules she mentions is the curfew, which she does not want to obey.

02-43

**Analyzing** Locate and underline the transition words and phrases used in the response.

**Deducing** Based on the information in the response, complete the following outline for the reading and the listening.

### Reading

Topic:

### Listening

Speaker's Opinion:

Reason 1:

Reason 2:

◈ **Reading** Read the following passage about the new dormitory opening on a university campus.

Reading Time: 45 Seconds

## New Dormitory Opening

City University is proud to announce the completion of Walker Hall, the newest addition to our student housing facilities. Rooms in Walker Hall will be available this fall. The dormitory offers the highest quality in student housing, with 140 sq. ft. private rooms, each with a private bathroom. Every floor is equipped with a kitchenette, a common area with a 47-inch flat-screen television, group study rooms, and laundry facilities. The cost to students is 14,000 dollars per academic year. This price includes unlimited use of the laundry machines as well as a meal plan at the cafeteria and the food court located on the first floor.

**(Checking)** Give a brief spoken response for each question.

**1** What is the purpose of the announcement?

**2** What features does the new dormitory have that make it special?

**3** What do students receive as part of the housing cost?

**4 Critical Thinking:** How might dormitory living differ from off-campus living?

◈ **Listening** Listen to two students as they discuss the above information and take notes.

┌─ • **Note** • ─────────────────────────────────────
│ **Speaker's Opinion:**
│
│                                                      02-44
│ Reason 1:
│
│
│ Reason 2:
│
└──────────────────────────────────────────────────

**Q** The woman expresses her opinion about the new dormitory building. Explain her opinion and the reasons she gives for holding it.

---

◆ **Planning** Plan your response by using the information from the reading and the listening.

**Her Opinion:**


Reason 1:


Reason 2:


**Transitions** *and* **Canned Phrases**

The woman will not live in the dorm because…       The woman thinks that apartments are…
She also feels that living off campus is…          Her first reason is that…
Instead of living in the dorm, she…                In addition to that, she says…


◆ **Speaking** Now give your spoken response for 60 seconds.

| Response time: 60 seconds | Your speaking time: _____ seconds |

## Task 3 | Psychology: Birth Order

---

**Vocabulary** Take a few moments to review the vocabulary items that will appear in this task.

**sibling** *n.* a brother or sister

**authoritative** *adj.* controlling; bossy

**out of place** *exp.* feeling different or not a part of something

**gratification** *n.* satisfaction; receiving what one wants

**profound** *adj.* significant; noteworthy

**phenomenon** *n.* a trend that occurs throughout a population

**overachiever** *n.* one who tries to have many accomplishments

**cognitive** *adj.* mental; of the mind

---

**Sample Response** | Prearrange your understanding of the task with the activities below.

The reading explains that birth order is when a person is born relative to his or her siblings, as in first-born, middle, youngest, and so forth. Some psychologists claim that first-born siblings have attributes of leadership and control while younger-born siblings are less likely to be overachievers and tend to dislike responsibility more. The professor confirms this assertion by presenting examples of sports figures and politicians. She names three first-born successes who are in the top ranks of their field while their younger siblings are much less accomplished. The professor goes on to say that birth order can affect not only people's personalities but also their intelligence. Citing recent research, she says that first-born siblings have an average of 2.3 more IQ points than their next-born siblings and that average IQs become lower as one goes down the birth order. This is attributed to the fact that first-born children must figure out how to do things by themselves and then go on to teach these things to their younger siblings.

02-45

**Analyzing** Locate and underline the transition words and phrases used in the response.

**Deducing** Based on the information in the sample response, complete the following outline about the reading and the listening.

**Reading**

Topic:

**Listening**

Main Idea:

Supporting Detail 1:

Supporting Detail 2:

## ◈ Reading Read the following passage about birth order and personality.

Reading Time: 45 Seconds

### Birth Order and Personality

Psychologists have long noted the differences in personality that can arise due to the order of one's birth relative to one's siblings. First-born children exhibit tendencies to become controlling, protective, or otherwise authoritative over younger siblings. Middle children are more likely to rebel from the family's expectations due to feeling out of place within the family. Youngest children demand more attention, dislike responsibility, and expect constant gratification. They are most similar to children without siblings, who are also used to being the center of attention and may feel they are being treated unfairly when things do not go their way.

**( Checking )** Give a brief spoken response for each question.

**1** According to the passage, what is birth order?

**2** How does being born first affect one's personality?

**3** In what way are youngest children similar to children without siblings?

**4 Critical Thinking:** Where does this passage fall in the nature vs. nurture debate?

## ◈ Listening Listen to a short lecture related to the reading. Take notes as needed.

---• Note •---

02-46

**Q** The professor explains how birth order influences people's lives. Using points and examples from the lecture, explain what birth order is and what effect it has on people.

---

◈ **Planning** Plan your response by using the information from the reading and the listening.

**Main Idea:**


Supporting Detail 1:


Supporting Detail 2:


**Transitions** *and* **Canned Phrases**

The passage explains that birth order is…          This is explained by the professor as…
In the lecture, we learn that…                      First-born siblings tend to be…
This is explained through the example of…          Birth order also affects…


◈ **Speaking** Now give your spoken response for 60 seconds.

| Response time: 60 seconds | Your speaking time: _____ seconds |
| --- | --- |

# Task 4 | Geology: Glacier Landforms

**Vocabulary** Take a few moments to review the vocabulary items that will appear in this task.

**retreat** *v.* to move back to the starting position

**indelible** *adj.* impossible to forget or to erase

**gigantic** *adj.* extremely large

**basin** *n.* a large bowl-shaped hole in the ground

**drain** *v.* to empty liquid from

**pebble** *n.* a small rock

**abrasive** *adj.* scratching and damaging with rough angles

**carve** *v.* to change the shape of something by cutting it

**Sample Response** | Prearrange your understanding of the task with the activities below.

The lecture is about how the retreat of glaciers during the last major ice age caused various land formations on the Earth today. The professor begins by explaining how the ice sheet that moved across North America created enormous lakes. The first example given is the Great Lakes, which are located on the border of the United States and Canada. The ice sheet knocked down mountains and made gigantic holes, which were later filled with melted ice. The second example is Lake Agassiz in the middle of Canada. It was formed by an ice sheet pressing down on the land. The professor then moves to some other landforms created by ice. These are the fjords of Norway and Iceland. As the ice retreated, it picked up rocks and pebbles, which gave it strong abrasive power. The ice tore up the land as it moved, creating interesting-looking fjords that we can see on maps today.

02-47

**Analyzing** Locate and underline the transition words and phrases used in the response.

**Deducing** Based on the information in the response, complete the following outline for the listening.

Topic:

Main Idea:

Supporting Detail 1:

Supporting Detail 2:

◈ **Listening** Listen to a short lecture and take notes.

┌─ • Note • ──────────────────────────────────────────┐
│                                                      │
│                                          [QR code]   │
│                                           02-48      │
│                                                      │
│                                                      │
│                                                      │
│                                                      │
│                                                      │
│                                                      │
└──────────────────────────────────────────────────────┘

**Q** The professor describes some effects of glaciers and ice sheets at the end of the last ice age. Using examples and details from the lecture, describe how the last ice age had a lasting effect on the Earth.

------------------------------------------------------------------------

◈ **Planning** Plan your response by using the information from the lecture.

**Main Idea:**


Supporting Detail 1:


Supporting Detail 2:


**Transitions** *and* **Canned Phrases**

The professor addresses the topic of…            As the glaciers retreated…
Ice sheets moved across the land, creating…      This movement resulted in the formation of…
The ice also affected the Earth by…              We can see its effects today in…


◈ **Speaking** Now give your spoken response for 60 seconds.

| Response time: 60 seconds | Your speaking time: _____ seconds |
|---|---|

# Task 1 | Living on or off Campus

**Q** Some students prefer to live on campus while others prefer to live in off-campus housing. Which do you prefer? Support your answer with reasons and examples.

◆ **Planning** Take 15 seconds to plan your answer.

**On Campus / Off Campus**

Supporting Detail 1:

Supporting Detail 2:

◆ **Speaking** Now give your spoken response for 45 seconds.

| Response time: 45 seconds | Your speaking time: _____ seconds |

**Transitions *and* Canned Phrases**

It would be best for me to live on campus because…

If I lived on campus, I could also…

Another reason I'd like to live off campus is…

I'd prefer to live off campus because…

◆ **Grading** Grade your response after you hear a sample response.

On Campus

02-49

Off Campus

02-50

| Score | 4 | 3 | 2 | 1 | Notes |
|---|---|---|---|---|---|
| Delivery | | | | | |
| Language | | | | | |
| Use | | | | | |
| Topic Development | | | | | |

# Task 2 | Increased Parking Permit Fees

**Vocabulary**   Take a few moments to review the vocabulary items that will appear in this task.

**first-come, first-served**  *exp.* given in order of request; unable to be reserved

**grant**  *v.* to give; to allow

**privilege**  *n.* a special right or benefit

**where does [one] get off**  *exp.* an expression of outrage

**free up**  *phr v.* to make available

**bingo**  *interj.* an expression of agreement or confirmation

**emission**  *n.* something released

**a drop in the bucket**  *exp.* a small amount

**◊ Reading**  You have 45 seconds to read the following passage.

Reading Time: 45 Seconds

## Changes to Parking Policy

Effective beginning in the fall semester, parking permit fees will increase by twenty-five percent for all students. Annual permits will be 300 dollars; semester permits will be 175 dollars. Lost or stolen permits can be replaced for a fee of 100 dollars. Permits may be purchased on a first-come, first-served basis at the Parking Services building. In addition, students residing in on-campus housing will no longer be granted on-campus parking privileges. The outside parking facility across from the campus main gate should be used instead.

**(Organizing)**  Fill out the following key points about the reading.

**Main Idea:**

Point 1:

Point 2:

**(Prediction)**  Based on the reading passage, predict what the speakers in the conversation will say.

**✔ Critical Thinking |**  What common goal do both parking-related changes share?

◊ **Listening** Now you will hear a short conversation related to the reading. Take notes about what both speakers say.

**• Note •**

Man:

02-51

Woman:

( **Critical Analysis** ) Give a brief spoken response to the following questions.

**1** How does the response compare to your prediction?

**2** What is another reason that could support the woman's opinion?

**3** How would you have reacted to the announcement?

**Q** The woman expresses her opinion about the changes to the parking permit policy. State her opinion and the reasons she gives for holding it.

---

◈ **Planning** Take 30 seconds to plan your answer.

**Woman's Opinion:**

Reason 1:

Reason 2:

**Transitions** *and* **Canned Phrases**

The woman is happy with/upset about the change in policy.

She also says that…
One reason she gives is that…

◈ **Speaking** Now give your spoken response for 60 seconds.

| Response time: 60 seconds | Your speaking time: _____ seconds |
|---|---|

◈ **Grading** Grade your response after you hear a sample response.

02-52

| Score | 4 | 3 | 2 | 1 | Notes |
|---|---|---|---|---|---|
| Delivery | | | | | |
| Language | | | | | |
| Use | | | | | |
| Topic Development | | | | | |

## Task 3 | Business: The Productivity Paradox

**Vocabulary** Take a few moments to review the vocabulary items that will appear in this task.

**implement** *v.* to put something into use

**countless** *adj.* too many to be counted; a great number of

**baffle** *v.* to confuse

**correlation** *n.* an association whereby a change in one affects something else

**social networking site** *n.* a website for connecting with friends

**fatigued** *adj.* tired

**boost** *v.* to increase

**comparable** *adj.* similar enough to be compared

◆ **Reading** You have 45 seconds to read the following passage.

Reading Time: 45 Seconds

### The Productivity Paradox and the Internet

When computer technology began to appear in offices across the nation, managers expected sharp increases in productivity. As it turns out, workplace productivity has seen no significant growth with the implementation of new technology. This phenomenon, called the productivity paradox, has inspired countless studies of office technology and, most recently, the Internet. Economists have been baffled by their findings. Nearly every office worker has access to the Internet now, and reports show that workers waste millions of hours each year playing online games and surfing the Web. Nevertheless, studies have demonstrated a strong correlation between Internet access and increased productivity.

**(Note Taking)** Fill out the following key points about the reading.

**Main Idea:**

Point 1:

Point 2:

**(Prediction)** Based on the reading passage, make a guess as to what the lecturer will say.

❤ **Critical Thinking |** Why do you think the Internet has increased workplace productivity?

◆ **Listening** Now you will hear a short lecture related to the reading. Take notes as you listen.

┌─ • **Note** • ─────────────────────────────────────────────┐
│                                                              │
│ **Main Idea:**                                    [QR code]  │
│                                                              │
│                                                    02-53     │
│ Supporting Detail 1:                                         │
│                                                              │
│                                                              │
│                                                              │
│ Supporting Detail 2:                                         │
│                                                              │
│                                                              │
│                                                              │
│                                                              │
└──────────────────────────────────────────────────────────────┘

(**Critical Analysis**) Give a brief spoken response to the following questions.

**1** How does the lecture compare to your prediction?

**2** Why might a new phone system or new electronic equipment slow down productivity?

**3** Are there any other technologies that you think might increase productivity?

**Q** The professor explains how the Internet has increased office productivity. Explain how the Internet increases productivity in spite of the productivity paradox.

◊ **Planning** Take 30 seconds to plan your answer.

**Main Idea:**

Supporting Detail 1:

Supporting Detail 2:

◊ **Speaking** Now give your spoken response for 60 seconds.

| Response time: 60 seconds | Your speaking time: _____ seconds |
|---|---|

◊ **Grading** Grade your response after you hear a sample response.

02-54

| Score | 4 | 3 | 2 | 1 | Notes |
|---|---|---|---|---|---|
| Delivery | | | | | |
| Language | | | | | |
| Use | | | | | |
| Topic Development | | | | | |

## Task 4 | The Arts: Dadaism

**Vocabulary** Take a few moments to review the vocabulary items that will appear in this task.

**blame** *v.* to assign guilt

**cultural elite** *exp.* the rich and powerful in society

**chaos** *n.* a lack of control and order

**presumably** *adv.* thought but not known for a fact

**troupe** *n.* a group or company of performers

**cause a stir** *exp.* to disrupt; to break the peace

**Listening** Listen to the following lecture about Dadaism. Take notes as you listen.

• Note •

**Main Idea:**

02-55

Supporting Detail 1:

Supporting Detail 2:

**Critical Analysis** Give a brief spoken response to the following questions.

**1** How does the professor explain the main point of the lecture?

**2** Based on the lecture, do you think the Dadaists were successful in their mission?

# Q

Using points and examples from the lecture, explain how and why the Dadaists fought back against the cultural elite of the early twentieth century.

---

◆ **Planning** You now have 20 seconds to plan your response.

**Main Idea:**

Supporting Detail 1:

Supporting Detail 2:

**Transitions** *and* **Canned Phrases**

The professor explains that the Dadaists fought against the cultural elite by…

As a result…

This caused…

The Dadaists did this by…

Another example of Dadaist resistance is…

◆ **Speaking** Now give your spoken response for 60 seconds.

| Response time: 60 seconds | Your speaking time: _____ seconds |
| --- | --- |

◆ **Grading** Grade your response after you hear a sample response.

02-56

| Score | 4 | 3 | 2 | 1 | Notes |
| --- | --- | --- | --- | --- | --- |
| Delivery | | | | | |
| Language | | | | | |
| Use | | | | | |
| Topic Development | | | | | |

**Chapter 08**

**Independent Speaking**

◊ Task 1  Movie Theaters or Home Viewing

**Integrated Speaking**

◊ Task 2  Dining with the University President

◊ Task 3  Health: Pandemics

◊ Task 4  Education: Literacy in Education

## Task 1 | Movie Theaters or Home Viewing

**Q** Do you prefer to watch movies at home or at movie theaters? Support your answer with details and examples.

---

### ◈ Planning Take 15 seconds to plan your answer.

**At Home / At Theaters**

Supporting Detail 1:

Supporting Detail 2:

### ◈ Speaking Now give your spoken response for 45 seconds.

| Response time: 45 seconds | Your speaking time: _____ seconds |
|---|---|

**Transitions and Canned Phrases**

In my opinion, it's better to watch a movie…　　　Watching movies at home is…
Movie theaters are better because…　　　To illustrate my point, one time…

### ◈ Grading Grade your response after you hear a sample response.

At Home　　　At Theaters

02-57　　　02-58

| Score | 4 | 3 | 2 | 1 | Notes |
|---|---|---|---|---|---|
| Delivery | | | | | |
| Language | | | | | |
| Use | | | | | |
| Topic Development | | | | | |

## Task 2 | Dining with the University President

**Vocabulary** Take a few moments to review the vocabulary items that will appear in this task.

**dine** *v.* to have a meal

**set aside** *v.* to reserve for a special purpose

**faculty** *n.* all of the teachers at a school

**pointless** *adj.* without importance or purpose

**inventor** *n.* a person who makes new things, particularly those based on technology

**improve** *v.* to make better

**◈ Reading** You have 45 seconds to read the following passage.

Reading Time: 45 Seconds

### All Students to Dine with University President

Starting in the spring semester, all students at the school will have the opportunity to dine with Enrico Medici, the president of the university. Mr. Medici will set aside time four days a week to have lunch or dinner with up to fifteen students at one time. All meals will be in the faculty dining hall in Dobson Hall. Students will be notified when they will be dining with Mr. Medici by e-mail. Students will have the opportunity to discuss campus life and anything else they wish to talk about with the president.

(**Note Taking**) Fill out the following key points about the reading.

**Main Idea:**

Point 1:

Point 2:

(**Prediction**) Based on the reading passage, predict what the speakers in the conversation will say.

✔ **Critical Thinking** | What would you like to discuss with your school's president if you had the chance?

◊ **Listening** Now you will hear a short conversation related to the reading. Take notes about what both speakers say.

**• Note •**

**Man:**

02-59

**Woman:**

**Critical Analysis** Give a brief spoken response to the following questions.

**1** How does the response compare to your prediction?

**2** How does the female speaker's opinion change in the conversation?

**3** What might the man want to talk about with the school president?

**Q** The man expresses his opinion about dining with the university president. State his opinion and the reasons he gives for holding it.

---

### ◆ Planning Take 30 seconds to plan your answer.

**Man's Opinion:**

Reason 1:

Reason 2:

### ◆ Speaking Now give your spoken response for 60 seconds.

| Response time: 60 seconds | Your speaking time: _____ seconds |
|---|---|

### ◆ Grading Grade your response after you hear a sample response.

02-60

| Score | 4 | 3 | 2 | 1 | Notes |
|---|---|---|---|---|---|
| Delivery | | | | | |
| Language | | | | | |
| Use | | | | | |
| Topic Development | | | | | |

# Task 3 | Health: Pandemics

---

**Vocabulary** Take a few moments to review the vocabulary items that will appear in this task.

**segment** *n.* a part; a portion

**novel** *adj.* new; never seen before

**immunity** *n.* a resistance to infection

**keep [something] in check** *exp.* to control the number or volume of something

**devastating** *adj.* having a severe and negative impact

**scholar** *n.* one who studies a subject in depth

**mingle** *v.* to mix with socially; to interact with

**tragedy** *n.* a sad situation

---

◆ **Reading** You have 45 seconds to read the following passage.

Reading Time: 45 Seconds

## Pandemics

A pandemic is the widespread occurrence of an infectious disease that affects great segments of populations across large areas of land, such as continents or even the entire world. A pandemic occurs when a novel disease is introduced to a population. Because it is novel, people do not have any natural immunity to it, so it spreads quickly throughout the population. Pandemics can have an incredible impact on a society—even to the point of completely wiping it out.

**(Note Taking)** Fill out the following key points about the reading.

**Main Idea:**

Point 1:

Point 2:

**(Prediction)** Based on the reading passage, make a guess as to what the lecturer will say.

✔ **Critical Thinking |** How could a novel disease be introduced into a population?

◊ **Listening** Now you will hear a short lecture related to the reading. Take notes as you listen.

**• Note •**

**Main Idea:**

02-61

Supporting Detail 1:

Supporting Detail 2:

**Critical Analysis** Give a brief spoken response to the following questions.

**1** How does the lecture compare to your prediction?

**2** What is the relationship between the reading and the listening?

**3** Are there any other pandemics that have occurred in modern times?

**Q** The professor explains pandemics with the example of the Spanish Flu. Using points and examples from the lecture, define pandemics, how they are spread, and what impact they have on societies.

---

◆ **Planning** Take 30 seconds to plan your answer.

**Main Idea:**

Supporting Detail 1:

Supporting Detail 2:

**Transitions *and* Canned Phrases**

A pandemic is a disease that…                  This is explained with the example of…
The flu was spread by…                         This caused the flu to…
The effect was felt by people in…              As a result, many people…

◆ **Speaking** Now give your spoken response for 60 seconds.

| Response time: 60 seconds | Your speaking time: _____ seconds |

◆ **Grading** Grade your response after you hear a sample response.

02-62

| Score | 4 | 3 | 2 | 1 | Notes |
|---|---|---|---|---|---|
| Delivery | | | | | |
| Language | | | | | |
| Use | | | | | |
| Topic Development | | | | | |

# Task 4 | Education: Literacy in Education

**Vocabulary** Take a few moments to review the vocabulary items that will appear in this task.

**epic** *adj.* extraordinarily lengthy

**chiefly** *adv.* primarily; mostly

**orally** *adv.* spoken

**cross-examination** *n.* a process of asking questions to determine truth

**crucial** *adj.* of the utmost importance

**coherently** *adv.* in a way that is clearly and effectively stated

**diminish** *v.* to lower

**be on to something** *exp.* to have a unique understanding of something

**Listening** Listen to the following lecture about literacy in education. Take notes as you listen.

**• Note •**

**Main Idea:**

02-63

Supporting Detail 1:

Supporting Detail 2:

**Critical Analysis**  Give a brief spoken response to the following questions.

1 Plato argued that literacy will diminish people's memory abilities. What positive effect does literacy have on people's overall breadth and depth of knowledge?

2 What is your opinion of Plato's argument that writing is "the third place from the truth"?

**Q** Using points and examples from the lecture, describe the educational model of Hellenic Greece and how and why some opposed the introduction of literacy.

---

◈ **Planning** You now have 20 seconds to plan your response.

**Main Idea:**


Supporting Detail 1:


Supporting Detail 2:

◈ **Speaking** Now give your spoken response for 60 seconds.

| Response time: 60 seconds | Your speaking time: _____ seconds |

◈ **Grading** Grade your response after you hear a sample response.

02-64

| Score | 4 | 3 | 2 | 1 | Notes |
|---|---|---|---|---|---|
| Delivery | | | | | |
| Language | | | | | |
| Use | | | | | |
| Topic Development | | | | | |

## Chapter 09

# Task 1 | Vacation Destinations

**Q** Some people prefer to travel to new destinations every vacation while others find one place they enjoy and return there often. Decide which you would prefer. Support your opinion with details and examples.

**Tip**

If you have not traveled much in your life, decide which option you would prefer if you traveled often and took regular vacations.

◈ **Planning** Take 15 seconds to plan your answer.

**New Destination / Same Destination**

Supporting Detail 1:

Supporting Detail 2:

◈ **Speaking** Now give your spoken response for 45 seconds.

| Response time: 45 seconds | Your speaking time: _____ seconds |
|---|---|

**Transitions** *and* **Canned Phrases**

I prefer to visit new places when I travel…
I find more happiness doing this because…

Every year, my family returns to…
This works better for us since…

◈ **Grading** Grade your response after you hear a sample response.

New Destination     Same Destination

02-65          02-66

| Score | 4 | 3 | 2 | 1 | Notes |
|---|---|---|---|---|---|
| Delivery | | | | | |
| Language | | | | | |
| Use | | | | | |
| Topic Development | | | | | |

# Task 2 | Department Budget Cuts

---

**Vocabulary** Take a few moments to review the vocabulary items that will appear in this task.

**deficit** *n.* a lack; an amount less than necessary

**fiscal year** *n.* a year-long period of accounting

**shortsighted** *adj.* showing poor judgment about the future

**disposal** *n.* the act of throwing away or removing

**minor** *n.* a secondary area of academic study

**inferior** *adj.* lesser in rank or importance

---

**Reading** You have 45 seconds to read the following passage.

Reading Time: 45 Seconds

## Do Not Cut Economics Budget

Because of a projected deficit for the coming fiscal year, each college was asked to cut twenty percent of its budget. I believe the College of Business has made a shortsighted decision to completely axe the Department of Economics. Some argue that our department was overstaffed, but if you look at registration figures, we have double the student credit hours of any other department. The complete disposal of our department will surely have negative effects on related majors as well as on the university's image and enrollment.

Regards,
*Geoffrey Ross*
Associate Professor of Economics

**Note Taking** Fill out the following key points about the reading.

**Main Idea:**

Point 1:

Point 2:

**Prediction** Based on the reading passage, predict what the speakers in the conversation will say.

❤**Critical Thinking |** How might cutting the Department of Economics from the budget negatively affect the university and its College of Business?

## ◊ Listening
Now you will hear a short conversation related to the reading. Take notes about what both speakers say.

> ┌─• **Note** •───────────────────────────────────┐
> │                                                │
> │  Man:                                  [QR]    │
> │                                       02-67    │
> │                                                │
> │                                                │
> │                                                │
> │  Woman:                                        │
> │                                                │
> │                                                │
> │                                                │
> └────────────────────────────────────────────────┘

**( Critical Analysis )** Give a brief spoken response to the following questions.

**1** How does the response compare to your prediction?

**2** How might the female student be affected by the change?

**3** What long-term effects could the change have on the College of Business's budget?

**Q** The woman expresses her opinion about the university cutting the Department of Economics. State her opinion and the reasons she gives for holding it.

---

◈ **Planning** Take 30 seconds to plan your answer.

**Woman's Opinion:**


Reason 1:


Reason 2:


**Transitions _and_ Canned Phrases**

| | |
|---|---|
| The woman is responding to an announcement about… | She thinks the change will disrupt… |
| The woman also feels that cutting the department will… | She thinks in the long run this will… |


◈ **Speaking** Now give your spoken response for 60 seconds.

| | | |
|---|---|---|
| Response time: 60 seconds | Your speaking time: _____ seconds | |


◈ **Grading** Grade your response after you hear a sample response.

02-68

| Score | 4 | 3 | 2 | 1 | Notes |
|---|---|---|---|---|---|
| Delivery | | | | | |
| Language | | | | | |
| Use | | | | | |
| Topic Development | | | | | |

## Task 3 | Economics: Monopoly Markets

---

**Vocabulary**  Take a few moments to review the vocabulary items that will appear in this task.

**competitive**  *adj.*  striving to defeat or outdo another

**profit**  *n.*  money that a person makes after spending is subtracted

**alternative**  *n.*  a possible other choice or action

**check out**  *v.*  to examine; to look at, often closely

**approximately**  *adv.*  around; about

**undesirable**  *adj.*  unwanted; disliked

---

◈ **Reading**  You have 45 seconds to read the following passage.

Reading Time: 45 Seconds

### Monopoly Markets

    Monopoly Markets exist in places where there is a single seller but many buyers. Because there is only one seller of a product, that person—called a monopolist—can charge any price. Buyers who want the product have no choice but to purchase it at the listed price. Most monopolists sell less than they would in competitive markets, but because they can charge high prices, they make large profits. In addition, buyers have no alternatives in monopoly markets, so if they are unwilling to deal with the monopolist, they cannot acquire the product.

**(Note Taking)**  Fill out the following key points about the reading.

**Main Idea:**

Point 1:

Point 2:

**(Prediction)**  Based on the reading passage, make a guess as to what the lecturer will say.

✔ **Critical Thinking |**  How might monopoly markets be harmful to buyers?

**◆ Listening** Now you will hear a short lecture related to the reading. Take notes as you listen.

---

**• Note •**

**Main Idea:**

02-69

Supporting Detail 1:

Supporting Detail 2:

---

**Critical Analysis** Give a brief spoken response to the following questions.

**1** How does the lecture compare to your prediction?

**2** Why does the professor discuss his personal experience at the airport?

**3** Elaborate on the professor's claims that monopoly markets are undesirable.

**Q** The professor describes a personal event from his life. Explain how it is related to monopoly markets.

--------------------------------------------------------------------------

◊ **Planning** Take 30 seconds to plan your answer.

**Main Idea:**


Supporting Detail 1:


Supporting Detail 2:


**Transitions *and* Canned Phrases**

The professor tells the students about…          He says he…
First, he noticed…                                Second, he saw that…
The situation at the airport is an example of…    This happens when…


◊ **Speaking** Now give your spoken response for 60 seconds.

| Response time: 60 seconds | Your speaking time: _____ seconds |


◊ **Grading** Grade your response after you hear a sample response.

02-70

| Score | 4 | 3 | 2 | 1 | Notes |
|---|---|---|---|---|---|
| Delivery | | | | | |
| Language | | | | | |
| Use | | | | | |
| Topic Development | | | | | |

# Task 4 | Geology: Dating Fossils

**Vocabulary**  Take a few moments to review the vocabulary items that will appear in this task.

**paleontologist**  *n.*  one who studies prehistoric life

**come up with**  *phr v.*  to think of; to devise

**fossil**  *n.*  the remains of something from the past

**crust**  *n.*  the outer layer of the Earth

**sediment**  *n.*  pieces of rock worn away from larger rocks

**lava**  *n.*  hot, melted rock that comes from the Earth's core

**come into play**  *exp.*  to become important

**isotope**  *n.*  atoms of the same element but with different numbers of neutrons

**radioactive**  *adj.*  unstable; easily bonding with other atoms

**decay**  *v.*  to wear away; to erode; to deteriorate

**Listening**  Listen to the following lecture about how fossils are dated. Take notes as you listen.

**• Note •**

**Main Idea:**

02-71

Supporting Detail 1:

Supporting Detail 2:

**Critical Analysis**  Give a brief spoken response to the following questions.

**1** How do you think strata are formed?

**2** Which of the two methods do you think is more similar to counting the rings of a tree? Why?

# Q Using points and details from the lecture, explain two methods of dating fossils.

◆ **Planning** You now have 20 seconds to plan your response.

**Main Idea:**

Supporting Detail 1:

Supporting Detail 2:

### Transitions *and* Canned Phrases

The professor begins by talking about…          The main idea of the lecture is that…
The first method discussed is…                       This process consists of…
The second way to date fossils is…                 Scientists use this to…

◆ **Speaking** Now give your spoken response for 60 seconds.

| Response time: 60 seconds | Your speaking time: _____ seconds |

◆ **Grading** Grade your response after you hear a sample response.

02-72

| Score | 4 | 3 | 2 | 1 | Notes |
|---|---|---|---|---|---|
| Delivery | | | | | |
| Language | | | | | |
| Use | | | | | |
| Topic Development | | | | | |

## Chapter 10

**Independent Speaking**

## Task 1 | Foreign Language Requirement

**Q** Many high schools require students to study a foreign language. Do you agree or disagree that knowledge of a foreign language should be a requirement for graduation? Include specific reasons and examples to support your answer.

> **Tip**
> Think of various ways that studying a foreign language does or does not benefit a person.

---

◆ **Planning** Take 15 seconds to plan your answer.

**Agree / Disagree**

Supporting Detail 1:

Supporting Detail 2:

◆ **Speaking** Now give your spoken response for 45 seconds.

| Response time: 45 seconds | Your speaking time: _____ seconds |
| --- | --- |

**Transitions and Canned Phrases**

I believe students should/should not have to…　　Studying a foreign language helps one to…
Besides that, foreign language study could…　　As an example…

◆ **Grading** Grade your response after you hear a sample response.

Agree　　　　Disagree

02-73　　　　02-74

| Score | 4 | 3 | 2 | 1 | Notes |
| --- | --- | --- | --- | --- | --- |
| Delivery | | | | | |
| Language | | | | | |
| Use | | | | | |
| Topic Development | | | | | |

# Task 2 │ New Cafeteria Meal Plans

**Vocabulary** Take a few moments to review the vocabulary items that will appear in this task.

**roll out**　*phr v.* to introduce a new plan or product

**flexibility**　*n.* an ability to change or be changed easily

**furnish**　*v.* to provide; to give

**archaic**　*adj.* ancient; very old

**exorbitant**　*adj.* more than what is fair; grossly expensive

**gouge**　*v.* to overcharge

**pricy**　*adj.* expensive

**cover**　*v.* to be enough to offset the cost of

◈**Reading** You have 45 seconds to read the following passage.

Reading Time: 45 Seconds

### New Cafeteria Meal Plans

The university cafeteria is happy to announce that we are rolling out a new meal plan for students starting this coming semester. The new meal plan will allow students to purchase only breakfast, lunch, or dinner on the plan. It will also let them mix and match any of the three. This will give more flexibility to students who may only wish to eat at the cafeteria once or twice a day. While the average meal price will rise by approximately one dollar, we believe this plan will furnish students with an overall better dining experience.

**(Note Taking)** Fill out the following key points about the reading.

**Main Idea:**

Point 1:

Point 2:

**(Prediction)** Based on the reading passage, predict what the speakers in the conversation will say.

✔**Critical Thinking |** How could the new plan end up saving students money even though it costs one dollar more per meal?

◆ **Listening** Now you will hear a short conversation related to the reading. Take notes about what both speakers say.

┌─ • **Note** • ──────────────────────────────────────────────────┐
│                                                                    │
│  **Man:**                                                 [QR code] │
│                                                            02-75    │
│                                                                    │
│                                                                    │
│                                                                    │
│  **Woman:**                                                        │
│                                                                    │
│                                                                    │
│                                                                    │
│                                                                    │
└────────────────────────────────────────────────────────────────────┘

( **Critical Analysis** ) Give a brief spoken response to the following questions.

**1** How does the response compare to your prediction?

**2** The woman mentions that most students she knows skip breakfast. Why might that be?

**3** What might be the reason for raising the price of meals at the cafeteria?

**Q** The woman expresses her opinion about the cafeteria's new meal plan. State her opinion and the reasons she gives for holding it.

◊ **Planning** Take 30 seconds to plan your answer.

**Woman's Opinion:**

Reason 1:

Reason 2:

**Transitions** *and* **Canned Phrases**

The woman feels that the new plan…          She thinks it will be helpful because…
She also states that the plan will allow her to…   Finally, she thinks she can save…

◊ **Speaking** Now give your spoken response for 60 seconds.

| Response time: 60 seconds | Your speaking time: _____ seconds |
|---|---|

◊ **Grading** Grade your response after you hear a sample response.

02-76

| Score | 4 | 3 | 2 | 1 | Notes |
|---|---|---|---|---|---|
| Delivery | | | | | |
| Language | | | | | |
| Use | | | | | |
| Topic Development | | | | | |

# Task 3 | Urban Studies: Urban Sprawl

---

**Vocabulary** Take a few moments to review the vocabulary items that will appear in this task.

**suburb** *n.* a small residential community outside a large city

**outskirts** *n.* outlying or bordering areas, such as of a city

**trend** *n.* a popular style

**boundary** *n.* something that indicates a limit

**impractical** *adj.* not useful

**prevalence** *n.* the condition of being widespread

**obesity** *n.* the condition of being very fat or overweight

**errand** *n.* a short trip with a specific purpose, such as buying groceries

**impervious** *adj.* not allowing penetration

**aquifer** *n.* an underground formation containing groundwater

---

◊ **Reading** You have 45 seconds to read the following passage.

Reading Time: 45 Seconds

## Urban Sprawl

Since the end of World War II, people in many developed nations, particularly the United States, have shown an increasing preference for residences in suburbs outside of or on the outskirts of cities. This trend, referred to as urban sprawl, occurs by way of converting rural farmland and countryside into residential or shopping areas. Because these suburban areas are highly regulated, areas of commerce, work, and industry are separated by distance and other boundaries, making public transportation impractical for most people. As a result, those involved in urban sprawl are highly dependent on personal vehicles.

**(Note Taking)** Fill out the following key points about the reading.

**Main Idea:**

Point 1:

Point 2:

**(Prediction)** Based on the reading passage, make a guess as to what the lecturer will say.

✔ **Critical Thinking |** What negative consequences might result from urban sprawl?

◈**Listening** Now you will hear a short lecture related to the reading. Take notes as you listen.

┌─ •**Note** •─────────────────────────────────────────────┐
│                                                                  │
│  **Main Idea:**                                    [QR code]     │
│                                                                  │
│                                                     02-77        │
│                                                                  │
│  Supporting Detail 1:                                            │
│                                                                  │
│                                                                  │
│                                                                  │
│                                                                  │
│  Supporting Detail 2:                                            │
│                                                                  │
│                                                                  │
│                                                                  │
│                                                                  │
│                                                                  │
│                                                                  │
└──────────────────────────────────────────────────────────┘

(**Critical Analysis**) Give a brief spoken response to the following questions.

**1** How does the lecture compare to your prediction?

**2** Why do you think suburbs are laid out the way they are with distance between each area?

**3** How might suburbs also affect the quality of water in underground water tables?

**Q** The professor explains urban sprawl and the negative effects it can have. Using points and examples from the lecture, define urban sprawl and explain how it can affect people's lives.

---

◆ **Planning** Take 30 seconds to plan your answer.

**Main Idea:**


Supporting Detail 1:


Supporting Detail 2:


**Transitions** *and* **Canned Phrases**

Urban sprawl is when…
The professor first mentions the problem of…
The other problem mentioned in the lecture is that of…

The professor explains the concept by…
This is caused by…
This results in…


◆ **Speaking** Now give your spoken response for 60 seconds.

| Response time: 60 seconds | Your speaking time: _____ seconds |
|---|---|


◆ **Grading** Grade your response after you hear a sample response.

02-78

| Score | 4 | 3 | 2 | 1 | Notes |
|---|---|---|---|---|---|
| Delivery | | | | | |
| Language | | | | | |
| Use | | | | | |
| Topic Development | | | | | |

## Task 4 | Agriculture: Crossbreeding

**Vocabulary** Take a few moments to review the vocabulary items that will appear in this task.

**weed out** *phr v.* to remove the weaker parts of a group

**desirable** *adj.* wanted; pleasing; worth having

**dime** *n.* a small coin worth ten cents

**settler** *n.* one who moves to and develops a new land

**famine** *n.* a widespread lack of food

**starvation** *n.* suffering and dying from a lack of food

**yield** *n.* the amount of something produced

**crisis** *n.* a situation that is unstable and problematic

**Listening** Listen to the following lecture about crossbreeding. Take notes as you listen.

• **Note** •

**Main Idea:**

02-79

Supporting Detail 1:

Supporting Detail 2:

**Critical Analysis** Give a brief spoken response to the following questions.

**1** How might wild strawberries differ from those that we find in grocery stores today?

**2** Explain how higher crop yields can stop famines and solve food crises.

**Q** Using points and details from the lecture, explain what crossbreeding is and how it is useful to humans.

---

◊ **Planning** You now have 20 seconds to plan your response.

**Main Idea:**

Supporting Detail 1:

Supporting Detail 2:

**Transitions** *and* **Canned Phrases**

| | |
|---|---|
| The professor is discussing the topic of… | This is defined as… |
| It is useful to humans first as a way to… | The professor uses the example of… |
| The other way crossbreeding is useful is… | This is explained with the example of… |

◊ **Speaking** Now give your spoken response for 60 seconds.

| Response time: 60 seconds | Your speaking time: _____ seconds |
|---|---|

◊ **Grading** Grade your response after you hear a sample response.

02-80

| Score | 4 | 3 | 2 | 1 | Notes |
|---|---|---|---|---|---|
| Delivery | | | | | |
| Language | | | | | |
| Use | | | | | |
| Topic Development | | | | | |

## Chapter 11

**Independent Speaking**

**Integrated Speaking**

## Task 1 | Purpose of University Study

**Q** Some people believe that the main purpose of attending university should be to prepare for a specific career. Do you agree or disagree? Include specific reasons and examples to support your answer.

---

◆ **Planning** Take 15 seconds to plan your answer.

**Agree / Disagree**

Supporting Detail 1:

Supporting Detail 2:

◆ **Speaking** Now give your spoken response for 45 seconds.

| Response time: 45 seconds | Your speaking time: _____ seconds |
| --- | --- |

**Transitions** *and* **Canned Phrases**

I agree that the primary purpose of university is to…    University does not necessarily have to…
The main reason I feel this way is that…    I'd also make the case that a degree can…

◆ **Grading** Grade your response after you hear a sample response.

Agree          Disagree

02-81          02-82

| Score | 4 | 3 | 2 | 1 | Notes |
| --- | --- | --- | --- | --- | --- |
| Delivery | | | | | |
| Language | | | | | |
| Use | | | | | |
| Topic Development | | | | | |

## Task 2 | Classes Relocated

---

**Vocabulary** Take a few moments to review the vocabulary items that will appear in this task.

**conduct** *v.* to carry out; to lead

**burden** *n.* a difficult task that often causes stress

**peeved** *adj.* annoyed; bothered

**sophomore** *n.* someone in his or her second year of study

**foundational** *adj.* basic; forming a base

**stellar** *adj.* extraordinarily good

---

◆ **Reading** You have 45 seconds to read the following passage.

Reading Time: 45 Seconds

### Classes Moved

Please be advised that our wing of the Engineering Department will be under construction for three weeks beginning Wednesday, March 13. During this time, I will not be able to conduct lectures in my normal classroom due to the disturbance created by the construction. Dr. Sanders, the Engineering Department chair, has arranged for us to meet in room 213 of the math and science building. It is just a basic classroom with no access to our regular computers and equipment, but in the end, we will have a much-improved engineering building. Thank you for your patience.

Regards,
*Dr. Angela Norris*
Professor of Engineering

**(Note Taking)** Fill out the following key points about the reading.

**Main Idea:**

Point 1:

Point 2:

**(Prediction)** Based on the reading passage, predict what the speakers in the conversation will say. Give your prediction as a brief, spoken response.

✔ **Critical Thinking |** What are the immediate downsides of the construction project?

◊**Listening** Now you will hear a short conversation related to the reading. Take notes about what both speakers say.

**• Note •**

Man:

02-83

Woman:

**( Critical Analysis )** Give a brief spoken response to the following questions.

**1** How does the response compare to your prediction?

**2** Does the man agree with the woman's main complaints?

**3** How will having better equipment put the students "ahead of the competition"?

**Q** The man expresses his opinion about the relocation of his engineering classes. State his opinion and the reasons he gives for holding it.

◈ **Planning** Take 30 seconds to plan your answer.

**Man's Opinion:**

Reason 1:

Reason 2:

**Transitions** *and* **Canned Phrases**

The man and the woman have just learned that…     The man thinks it is a convenience since…
He also thinks the changes will benefit him by…     …which is why he is happy about the change.

◈ **Speaking** Now give your spoken response for 60 seconds.

| Response time: 60 seconds | Your speaking time: _____ seconds |
|---|---|

◈ **Grading** Grade your response after you hear a sample response.

02-84

| Score | 4 | 3 | 2 | 1 | Notes |
|---|---|---|---|---|---|
| Delivery | | | | | |
| Language | | | | | |
| Use | | | | | |
| Topic Development | | | | | |

## Task 3 | Earth Science: Biodiversity

**Vocabulary** Take a few moments to review the vocabulary items that will appear in this task.

**meticulously** *adv.* with great attention to detail

**catalogue** *v.* to make a list of

**myriad** *n.* a great selection; a large number

**stability** *n.* the condition of being self-supportive and balanced

**shoot [oneself] in the foot** *exp.* to do something to hurt oneself

**alarming** *adj.* causing worry; worthy of immediate attention

**fetch a high price** *exp.* to sell for a lot of money

**habitat** *n.* a natural environment of a species

**endemic** *adj.* naturally occurring in a location

**dwindle** *v.* slowly and gradually to be reduced

**Reading** You have 45 seconds to read the following passage.

Reading Time: 45 Seconds

### Biodiversity

The sum of all living organisms on the planet is what biologists call biodiversity. To date, scientists have meticulously catalogued just over 1.4 million species of plants, animals, and bacteria, which represent only a fraction of the estimated ten to thirty million species that exist on the Earth. Biodiversity is important not only to individual ecosystems but also to humanity by providing a myriad of medicinal and food resources as well as by inspiring art and by contributing to climate stability.

**(Note Taking)** Fill out the following key points about the reading.

**Main Idea:**

Point 1:

Point 2:

**(Prediction)** Based on the reading passage, make a guess as to what the lecturer will say. Give your prediction as a brief, spoken response.

**✔Critical Thinking |** How does biodiversity contribute to climate stability?

◆ **Listening** Now you will hear a short lecture related to the reading. Take notes as you listen.

---

**• Note •**

**Main Idea:**

02-85

Supporting Detail 1:

Supporting Detail 2:

---

( **Critical Analysis** ) Give a brief spoken response to the following questions.

**1** How does the lecture compare to your prediction?

**2** What does the professor mean by saying that we humans are "shooting ourselves in the foot"?

**3** Why does the professor say that habitat loss is more destructive than overhunting?

**Q** The professor explains how human activity is damaging biodiversity. Using points and examples from the lecture, define biodiversity and explain what humans are doing to hurt it.

---

◆ **Planning** Take 30 seconds to plan your answer.

**Main Idea:**

Supporting Detail 1:

Supporting Detail 2:

**Transitions *and* Canned Phrases**

Biodiversity is defined as the sum of…          The lecture explains that humans are…
This is happening first by way of…              This damages biodiversity by…
Humans are also guilty of…                      When we do this, mobile organisms…

◆ **Speaking** Now give your spoken response for 60 seconds.

| Response time: 60 seconds | Your speaking time: _____ seconds |
|---|---|

◆ **Grading** Grade your response after you hear a sample response.

02-86

| Score | 4 | 3 | 2 | 1 | Notes |
|---|---|---|---|---|---|
| Delivery | | | | | |
| Language | | | | | |
| Use | | | | | |
| Topic Development | | | | | |

# Task 4 | Chemistry: Electron Configuration

**Vocabulary** Take a few moments to review the vocabulary items that will appear in this task.

**atom** *n.* the smallest unit of an element

**neutron** *n.* a subatomic particle with no charge

**proton** *n.* a subatomic particle with a positive charge

**electron** *n.* a subatomic particle with a negative charge

**configuration** *n.* the way that something is arranged

**orbit** *v.* to travel in a circular path around an object

**nucleus** *n.* the central part of an atom, which is composed of protons and neutrons

**valence** *n.* the ability of an atom to combine with other atoms

**compound** *n.* a combination of two or more items

**◊ Listening** Listen to the following lecture about electron configuration. Take notes as you listen.

**• Note •**

**Main Idea:**

02-87

Supporting Detail 1:

Supporting Detail 2:

**(Critical Analysis)** Give a brief spoken response to the following questions.

**1** Why does the professor not explain how many electrons are in each shell?

**2** Based on the information in the lecture, what type of atom would be best for making compounds?

**Q** Using points and details from the lecture, explain electron configuration and why it is important in chemistry.

◊ **Planning** You now have 20 seconds to plan your response.

**Main Idea:**

Supporting Detail 1:

Supporting Detail 2:

**Transitions** *and* **Canned Phrases**

The professor's lecture is focused on…          This is defined as…
The professor explains that electron shells are…   These shells can affect…
The reason it is important is that…              In other words, valence shells affect…

◊ **Speaking** Now give your spoken response for 60 seconds.

| Response time: 60 seconds | Your speaking time: _____ seconds |
| --- | --- |

◊ **Grading** Grade your response after you hear a sample response.

02-88

| Score | 4 | 3 | 2 | 1 | Notes |
| --- | --- | --- | --- | --- | --- |
| Delivery | | | | | |
| Language | | | | | |
| Use | | | | | |
| Topic Development | | | | | |

**Chapter 12**

**Independent Speaking**

## Task 1 | Public Funding of Museums

**Q** Some people think that art museums should be funded by the government while others believe they should be funded privately. Which do you prefer? Include reasons and details to support your opinion.

◆ **Planning** Take 15 seconds to plan your answer.

**Public / Private Funding**

Supporting Detail 1:

Supporting Detail 2:

◆ **Speaking** Now give your spoken response for 45 seconds.

| Response time: 45 seconds | Your speaking time: _____ seconds |
| --- | --- |

**Transitions _and_ Canned Phrases**

In my view, art should be funded by…
First and foremost, art is something that…

I don't believe that the government should…
Besides that, I think that art…

◆ **Grading** Grade your response after you hear a sample response.

Public                    Private Funding

02-89

02-90

| Score | 4 | 3 | 2 | 1 | Notes |
| --- | --- | --- | --- | --- | --- |
| Delivery | | | | | |
| Language | | | | | |
| Use | | | | | |
| Topic Development | | | | | |

## Task 2 | Controversial Speaker

---

**Vocabulary** Take a few moments to review the vocabulary items that will appear in this task.

**controversial** *adj.* causing debate

**radical** *adj.* outside the mainstream; extreme

**dismayed** *adj.* disappointed; upset

**forum** *n.* a place to speak and give one's opinion

**all around** *exp.* in every way

**all for** *exp.* in favor of; in support of

**shun** *v.* to reject from a social group

**activism** *n.* the active promotion of an idea or goal

---

❖**Reading** You have 45 seconds to read the following passage.

Reading Time: 45 Seconds

### Letter to the Editor

Like many of the people I have talked to, I was very disappointed to read in last week's paper that the university has decided to allow the controversial figure Melvin Harper to give a speech here next month. Mr. Harper is the leader of a radical environmentalism organization that has been linked to domestic terrorist activities. Besides that, he has been criticized severely in the news media for spreading mistruths about environmental problems and policies. I am truly dismayed by our university's decision to give him a public forum.

*Mary Ann Beckworth*
Junior in Biology

**(Note Taking)** Fill out the following key points about the reading.

**Main Idea:**

Point 1:

Point 2:

**(Prediction)** Based on the reading passage, predict what the speakers in the conversation will say. Give your prediction as a brief, spoken response.

❤**Critical Thinking |** What argument could be made for allowing controversial figures to speak at a university?

♦ **Listening** Now you will hear a short conversation related to the reading. Take notes about what both speakers say.

**• Note •**

Man:

02-91

Woman:

( **Critical Analysis** ) Give a brief spoken response to the following questions.

**1** How does the response compare to your prediction?

**2** Why does the man think Mr. Harper should be shunned?

**3** What does the woman mean when she says shunning Mr. Harper would be thought control?

# Q The woman expresses her opinion about allowing a controversial figure to speak at her university. State her opinion and the reasons she gives for holding it.

◆ **Planning** Take 30 seconds to plan your answer.

**Woman's Opinion:**

Reason 1:

Reason 2:

**Transitions** and **Canned Phrases**

The woman is expressing her opinion about…    She believes the speaker should be allowed…
She begins by saying that…                    She also feels that the speaker will…

◆ **Speaking** Now give your spoken response for 60 seconds.

| Response time: 60 seconds | Your speaking time: _____ seconds |
|---|---|

◆ **Grading** Grade your response after you hear a sample response.

02-92

| Score | 4 | 3 | 2 | 1 | Notes |
|---|---|---|---|---|---|
| Delivery | | | | | |
| Language | | | | | |
| Use | | | | | |
| Topic Development | | | | | |

## Task **3** | American History: The Temperance Movement

---

**Vocabulary** Take a few moments to review the vocabulary items that will appear in this task.

**spring up** *phr v.* to arise; to come into existence

**abstinence** *n.* the practice of not doing something

**abolition** *n.* the act of doing away with or removing

**mainstream** *adj.* popular; representing a dominant idea or belief

**rid** *v.* to remove; to make free from

**tavern** *n.* a location that serves alcoholic beverages

**fringe** *n.* the outer edge; outside of the mainstream

**hymn** *n.* a religious song praising or thanking a deity

---

**◊ Reading** You have 45 seconds to read the following passage.

Reading Time: 45 Seconds

### The American Temperance Movement

As early as 1789, various groups began to spring up around the American northeast with the goal of discouraging heavy drinking in their local areas. The movement began with the modest aims of temperance, which is the promotion of only moderate drinking, and voluntary abstinence, but it eventually grew to advocate the complete abolition of alcohol from society. With several million followers by the twentieth century, the movement had the political power necessary to push for legal action to achieve its aims, resulting in the legal prohibition of alcohol from 1919 to 1933.

**(Note Taking)** Fill out the following key points about the reading.

**Main Idea:**

Point 1:

Point 2:

**(Prediction)** Based on the reading passage, make a guess as to what the lecturer will say. Give your prediction as a brief, spoken response.

**✔ Critical Thinking |** What measures might the followers of the temperance movement have taken to achieve their political goals?

◆ **Listening** Now you will hear a short lecture related to the reading. Take notes as you listen.

┌─────────────────────────────────────────────────────────────┐
**• Note •**

**Main Idea:**


**Supporting Detail 1:**



**Supporting Detail 2:**


02-93
└─────────────────────────────────────────────────────────────┘

**Critical Analysis** Give a brief spoken response to the following questions.

**1** How does the lecture compare to your prediction?

**2** Based on the information in the lecture, what do you think may have inspired Carrie Nation to act?

**3** Why does the professor point out that Carrie Nation was not a leader?

**Q** The professor explains the role that women played in the American Temperance Movement. Using points and examples from the lecture, explain what the American Temperance Movement was and how women played a role in its growth.

---

◈ **Planning** Take 30 seconds to plan your answer.

**Main Idea:**

Supporting Detail 1:

Supporting Detail 2:

**Transitions** *and* **Canned Phrases**

The American Temperance Movement began with…    The professor points out that women…
Her first example is of…    But not all supporters were radical…
She goes on to describe how…    The professor finishes by saying…

◈ **Speaking** Now give your spoken response for 60 seconds.

| Response time: 60 seconds | Your speaking time: _____ seconds |

◈ **Grading** Grade your response after you hear a sample response.

02-94

| Score | 4 | 3 | 2 | 1 | Notes |
|---|---|---|---|---|---|
| Delivery | | | | | |
| Language | | | | | |
| Use | | | | | |
| Topic Development | | | | | |

Task **4**  **Health: Diabetes**

**Vocabulary**  Take a few moments to review the vocabulary items that will appear in this task.

**overview**  *n.* a summary; a general review

**glucose**  *n.* sugar used by the body

**hormone**  *n.* a substance produced by the body

**pancreas**  *n.* an internal organ that processes glucose

**insufficient**  *adj.* not enough

**regimen**  *n.* a detailed plan of action

**symptom**  *n.* a sign that indicates disease or illness

**fatigue**  *n.* the state of having very little energy

**abnormal**  *adj.* unusual; not normal

**numbness**  *n.* a partial or total lack of feeling in the body

◊ **Listening**  Listen to the following lecture about diabetes. Take notes as you listen.

**• Note •**

**Main Idea:**

02-95

Supporting Detail 1:

Supporting Detail 2:

(**Critical Analysis**)  Give a brief spoken response to the following questions.

**1** How does the professor organize the lecture?

**2** Why does the professor say that some symptoms are hidden?

# Q Using points and details from the lecture, explain what diabetes is and what effects it can have on a person.

◈ **Planning** You now have 20 seconds to plan your response.

**Main Idea:**

Supporting Detail 1:

Supporting Detail 2:

### Transitions *and* Canned Phrases

| | |
|---|---|
| The topic of the lecture is… | The professor starts by defining… |
| He explains further by defining two types… | This type is defined by… |
| The professor goes on to explain the symptoms… | While some symptoms are easily noticed… |

◈ **Speaking** Now give your spoken response for 60 seconds.

| | |
|---|---|
| Response time: 60 seconds | Your speaking time: _____ seconds |

◈ **Grading** Grade your response after you hear a sample response.

02-96

| Score | 4 | 3 | 2 | 1 | Notes |
|---|---|---|---|---|---|
| Delivery | | | | | |
| Language | | | | | |
| Use | | | | | |
| Topic Development | | | | | |

# Part

# C

# Experiencing the TOEFL iBT Actual Tests

# Actual Test 01

## Speaking Section Directions

03-01

 Make sure your headset is on.

This section measures your ability to speak about a variety of topics. You will answer four questions by speaking into the microphone. Answer as completely as possible.

In the first question, you will speak about familiar topics. Your response will be scored on your ability to speak clearly and coherently.

In the next two questions, you will first read a short reading passage. This passage will go away, and you will then listen to a talk on the same topic. You will be asked about the information you have read and heard. You will need to combine information from the reading passage and the talk to provide a complete answer. Your response will be scored on your ability to speak clearly and coherently and how accurately you convey information about what you read and heard.

In the last question, you will listen to part of a lecture. You will be asked about what you have heard. Your response will be scored on your ability to speak clearly and coherently and how accurately you convey information about what you heard.

You may take notes while you read and while you listen to the conversations and lectures. You may use your notes to help prepare your response.

Listen carefully to the directions for each question. The directions will not be written on the screen.

For each question you will be given a short time to prepare your response (15 to 30 seconds, depending on the question). A clock will show how much preparation time is remaining. When the preparation time is up, you will be told to begin your response. A clock will show how much response time is remaining. A message will appear on the screen when the response time has ended.

## Task 1

03-02

Some people think students should be involved in extracurricular activities. Others think that students should concentrate only on academics. Which opinion do you support? Include specific reasons and examples to support your answer.

| PREPARATION TIME |
|:---:|
| 00:00:15 |

| RESPONSE TIME |
|:---:|
| 00:00:45 |

## Task 2

03-03

### Rosemary Hall to Become Freshman Only

As of the fall semester, Rosemary Hall, which is located next to Barnum Hall on the eastern side of the campus, will be reserved only for first-year students. Up until now, Rosemary Hall has housed freshmen, sophomores, and juniors. The change has been instituted thanks to recent comments by freshmen students expressing a desire to have a dormitory reserved solely for them. Rosemary Hall features 120 double rooms, ten triple rooms, and sixty-five single rooms. Incoming students interested in living in the dormitory should make their desire known to the student housing office.

The woman expresses her opinion regarding Rosemary Hall. State her opinion and explain the reasons she gives for holding that opinion.

| PREPARATION TIME |
|:---:|
| 00:00:30 |

| RESPONSE TIME |
|:---:|
| 00:00:60 |

# Task 3

03-04

## The Hawthorne Effect

During the period from 1924 to 1932, a series of experiments were conducted at a factory called Hawthorne Works. The experiments were part of a study on worker productivity, specifically how changes in the workplace environment could affect output levels in a telephone-assembly room. The researchers found that any manipulation of the factory, management, or schedule positively influenced both individual and overall output. In the end, however, the study demonstrated that it was not changes in the environment that influenced output but simply the fact that the workers knew they were being monitored.

The professor explains the Hawthorne Effect by describing a study and comparing the researchers' initial findings to their later conclusions. Describe these differences.

| PREPARATION TIME |
| :---: |
| 00:00:30 |

| RESPONSE TIME |
| :---: |
| 00:00:60 |

# Task 4

03-05

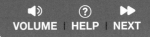
Using points and examples from the lecture, explain what working animals are and the various ways in which they are used by humans.

| PREPARATION TIME |
|:---:|
| 00:00:20 |

| RESPONSE TIME |
|:---:|
| 00:00:60 |

## Speaking Section Directions

03-06

 Make sure your headset is on.

This section measures your ability to speak about a variety of topics. You will answer four questions by speaking into the microphone. Answer as completely as possible.

In the first question, you will speak about familiar topics. Your response will be scored on your ability to speak clearly and coherently.

In the next two questions, you will first read a short reading passage. This passage will go away, and you will then listen to a talk on the same topic. You will be asked about the information you have read and heard. You will need to combine information from the reading passage and the talk to provide a complete answer. Your response will be scored on your ability to speak clearly and coherently and how accurately you convey information about what you read and heard.

In the last question, you will listen to part of a lecture. You will be asked about what you have heard. Your response will be scored on your ability to speak clearly and coherently and how accurately you convey information about what you heard.

You may take notes while you read and while you listen to the conversations and lectures. You may use your notes to help prepare your response.

Listen carefully to the directions for each question. The directions will not be written on the screen.

For each question you will be given a short time to prepare your response (15 to 30 seconds, depending on the question). A clock will show how much preparation time is remaining. When the preparation time is up, you will be told to begin your response. A clock will show how much response time is remaining. A message will appear on the screen when the response time has ended.

# Task 1

03-07

Do you agree or disagree with the following statement? To understand another country's culture, you must first understand its language. Give specific reasons and examples to support your opinion.

| PREPARATION TIME |
|:---:|
| 00:00:15 |

| RESPONSE TIME |
|:---:|
| 00:00:45 |

## Task 2

03-08

### New Laundry Facility

City University is pleased to announce that construction on the new laundry facility has been completed. The new facility, located directly across from Perkins Hall, will open today. The existing facility will be shut down and used for other purposes. The new facility will feature washing machines that can handle twenty pounds of laundry at a time. This is up from the twelve pounds that the existing machines can handle. The price per use will rise from seventy-five cents to 1.25 dollars per load, but with the higher capacity, the overall price per pound will not change.

The woman expresses her opinion regarding the opening of the new laundry facility. State her opinion and explain the reasons she gives for holding that opinion.

| PREPARATION TIME |
| --- |
| 00:00:30 |

| RESPONSE TIME |
| --- |
| 00:00:60 |

# Task 3

03-09

## Logical Fallacies

In studying logic and philosophy, it is important to be able to recognize and deal with flaws in an argument. These flaws, known as logical fallacies, may occur by mistake or by intention. There are dozens of types of logical fallacies, and each works in a different way to confuse or distract the reader or even to cause an argument to become invalid. A keen reader of philosophy should be aware of and able to detect a wide range of logical fallacies, particularly those which most commonly appear in logical debates.

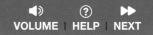
The professor explains logical fallacies by discussing the strawman fallacy. Describe the strawman fallacy and explain how it is used.

| PREPARATION TIME |
|:---:|
| 00:00:30 |

| RESPONSE TIME |
|:---:|
| 00:00:60 |

# Task 4

03-10

Using points and examples from the lecture, describe the two primary categories of motivation.

| PREPARATION TIME |
|:---:|
| 00:00:20 |

| RESPONSE TIME |
|:---:|
| 00:00:60 |

Memo

Memo

# TOEFL® MAP Speaking

**New TOEFL® Edition**

Advanced

## Scripts and Answer Key

# TOEFL® MAP
## MAP Speaking
### New TOEFL® Edition

**Advanced**

**Scripts and Answer Key**

# Part B-1
## Building Knowledge & Skills for the Speaking Test

## Task 1 | Choosing a Career

### ◊ Planning                                              p.30

▷ **Don't Rely on Advice**

Supporting Detail 1: *No one truly knows my passions.*

Supporting Detail 2: *Individual responsibility*

▷ **Rely on Advice**

Supporting Detail 1: *experienced people – provide insight about careers*

Supporting Detail 2: *others can judge my personality*

### ◊ Comparing                                              p.30

**Sample Response 1** Don't Rely on Advice          02-01

I feel that when making important decisions such as what career to pursue, we should not depend on the advice of others. For one thing, I think that no one can ever truly know what my passions and interests are. I'm a naturally quiet and reserved person, and that may lead someone to recommend a desk job, such as in a quiet office or library. But the truth is that I thrive on teamwork and group cooperation. The other reason I wouldn't seek other people's advice is that I believe all people are responsible for their own lives. Just as I would not expect others to help me decide what car to drive or what to have for dinner, I cannot expect anyone else to choose my career for me. It's something we must each decide for ourselves.

**Sample Response 2** Rely on Advice                 02-02

I believe that we should consider the advice of others before deciding on a career. To me, the most obvious reason is that other people may have experience in the career field that I have in mind. Someone with years of experience would obviously have insight into the actual day-to-day routine of a job. Thus, that person would be able to give me inside information and help me make a more informed decision. On top of that, other people might be able to help me determine if I have the right personality for a particular career. If they think I'm not suited for a particular career, they could prevent me from making a bad choice that I would eventually regret.

## Task 2 | New Student Activities Fee

### Sample Response                                         p.31
**Analyzing**

The announcement states that the university's student activities fee will be increased from seventy-five to 100 dollars because of the economy. The fee funds various student activities and organizations, but it is not mandatory, and students can opt out of it. The man is upset about the increase and says there is no way he will pay it. The first reason for his opinion is that he reads the newspaper but does not make use of the other things the fee funds, such as student activities and athletic clubs. He also stresses that he cannot afford the increase by saying that the fee would require him to work more hours at his job. Even though the female student points out that fifty dollars is small compared to the annual tuition, the male student says that it would be five more hours of work for something that does not benefit him.

**Deducing**

**Reading**

Topic: *increased student activities fee*

**Listening**

Speaker's Opinion: *The man is unhappy about it.*

Reason 1: *doesn't make use of the campus activities*

Reason 2: *cannot afford the extra $50*

### ◊ Reading                                               p.35
**Checking**

1   The fee increase is in response to current economic conditions.

2   The fee funds the student newspaper, the amateur literary magazine, athletics clubs, the student recreation center, and annual student events such as the Spring Fling.

3   Students who don't want to pay the fee can fill out a waiver at the Finance Office.

4   **Critical Thinking:** Someone might not pay the fee because that person doesn't have enough money or because the person is upset about the increased cost.

M: Can you believe they raised the student activities fee by fifty dollars? There's no way I'm paying that.

W: No one likes paying extra fees, but it's not as if we don't benefit from it. You see, it funds so many things that we all use.

M: But I don't use any of those things. I commute, and I definitely don't stick around any longer than I have to.

W: But you read the student newspaper and go to the events, right?

M: Well, I do read the paper, but I've got no interest in the Spring Fling or anything else. I'm only here at the university to learn. I can socialize on my own terms.

W: Okay, but it's only fifty dollars more than last year. Considering tuition is 8,000 dollars a year, I don't think it's much to ask.

M: You're missing the point. I don't have any financial aid, and you know I work to put myself through college. That fifty dollars represents another few hours I have to work, and for what?

W: I suppose you're free to do what you want, but I think everyone should chip in. It's only fair.

◈ **Planning** p.33

**His Opinion:** *He does not want to pay the fee.*

Reason 1: *He does not make use of the activities that the activities fee funds.*

Reason 2: *He cannot afford to pay any extra money because he doesn't receive financial aid and puts himself through college with money from his job.*

Chapter **01** | Integrated Speaking

Task **3** | **Anthropology: Early Civilizations**

**Sample Response** p.34

**Analyzing**

The reading states that human civilization arose after the rise of agriculture in 9500 B.C. and claims that the Indus Valley Civilization was remarkable for its technological advancements, especially in science and urban planning. The professor explains further by giving two examples of advanced technology in the Indus Valley Civilization. The professor begins by describing how urban planning was

used in that civilization. He says that even though the people lived in densely populated urban areas, they were not unsanitary. The reason is that the cities had advanced pipe systems, which allowed sewage systems to be built and water to be piped into everyone's home. The professor also points out that the intricate measuring system allowed for perfect ratios in building bricks. These examples show what the Indus Valley Civilization had urban planning and measuring systems superior to any of that time period, which makes it remarkable and unique.

**Deducing**

**Reading**

Topic: *Indus Valley Civilization*

**Listening**

Main Idea: *advanced urban planning and science*

Supporting Detail 1: *advanced pipe systems*

Supporting Detail 2: *precise measurements for engineering*

◈ **Reading** p.35

**Checking**

1   People shifted from being hunter-gatherers to living in small agrarian communities.

2   They had unified communities that exhibited advanced arts, materials development, and record keeping.

3   Its advancements in science and urban planning were remarkable.

4   **Critical Thinking:** Archaeology and anthropology help us understand the mistakes people in the past made so that we may avoid them.

◈ **Listening** p.35

Script 02-06

**Professor:** We talked before about the advancements in arts and architecture made by the Mesopotamians and Egyptians. Today, let's turn our attention to the Indus Valley region. Since the Indus Valley Civilization consisted of densely populated cities, one might expect they were unsanitary slums like modern ghettos or trench towns. But in fact, quite the opposite was true. Indus Valley cities featured the world's first urban sanitation systems. The common house was equipped with a private well for drawing water for drinking and bathing as well as a drainage pipe that led out to a covered sewage system. Their plumbing and drainage systems, designed some 5,000 years ago, surpassed some existing even today in Pakistan and India.

But their brilliance didn't end with urban planning. Their scientific and engineering feats were extremely impressive, too. The bricks used for construction were of a perfect 4:2:1 ratio, each having uniform dimensions and weights. This was made possible by their intricate measuring system, the smallest unit of which was equal to 1.704 mm. This was the smallest unit of measurement from the Bronze Age, and it indicates a high degree of accuracy in their engineering. As a result, their docks, granaries, and walls were the sturdiest during that era.

## ◈ Planning

p.36

**Main Idea:** *The Indus Valley Civilization was remarkable for its time.*

Supporting Detail 1: *urban planning – excellent pipes and sewage systems*

Supporting Detail 2: *engineering – precise measurements (1.704mm) and advanced buildings*

Chapter **01** | Integrated Speaking

## Task 4 | Economics: The Labor Theory of Value

## Sample Response

p.37

**Analyzing**

The professor explains the labor theory of value by explaining the positions of Adam Smith and Karl Marx. Adam Smith stated that products' costs should be determined by how much labor was required to produce them, not by market forces. To illustrate this, the professor gives an example of cars and motorcycles. If cars take three times more work to produce than motorcycles do, then cars should be three times as expensive. However, Smith said that capitalism should take over after a society advances. In contrast, Karl Marx believed the labor theory of value should always take the place of capitalism. He argued that labor power is not paid fairly by capitalists. In other words, workers are exploited by capitalists. As an example, Marx said that if workers in a factory were paid a fair salary, then profits would be impossible. So while Smith and Marx disagreed on some details, they both believed in using labor to determine a product's value.

**Deducing**

Topic: *labor theory of value*

Main Idea: *Value is determined by the work required.*

Supporting Detail 1: *Adam Smith – products that require more work should be more expensive, e.g. cars and motorcycles*

Supporting Detail 2: *Karl Marx – labor theory of value should replace capitalism; capitalists exploit workers and pay unfair wages*

## ◈ Listening

p.38

Script 02-08

**Professor:** How much do you value a new pair of sneakers? Are they worth fifty dollars to you? 150 dollars? It probably depends on the brand name and the quality of the shoes, right? These are just a couple of factors that determine value in modern mainstream economics. But in studying current theory, we must make sure that we understand some foundational concepts.

Adam Smith talked about something called the labor theory of value. Rather than allowing market forces to determine the value—or cost—of a product, the amount of labor involved in the production process should instead be the deciding factor. To give you an idea of what this means, imagine that a car takes three times longer to produce than a motorcycle. Then the prices of cars will always be triple the prices of motorcycles. Now, Smith saw this as a fine model for primitive societies but saw capitalist influences, such as the sale of stock, taking its place as a society advances.

Karl Marx, on the other hand, believed the labor theory to be superior to capitalist theories of value. He argued that labor theory could explain the value of all commodities, including the value of a worker's labor, which he sells to a factory, for example. This is where we get the term labor power today. Capitalists, Marx argued, did not pay workers a fair wage for their labor power. This is where he supposed profits came from: the exploitation of workers. If workers were paid the true value of their labor, then profits would be impossible. That's according to Marx, at least.

**Main Idea:** *Some thinkers prefer labor the theory of value.*

Supporting Detail 1: *Adam Smith → young societies only; pay cost equal to labor required for production*

Supporting Detail 2: *Karl Marx → labor theory > capitalism; capitalism exploits workers*

---

Chapter **02** | Independent Speaking

## Task 1 | Exams vs. Coursework

### ◊ Planning p.40

▷ **Examinations**

Supporting Detail 1: *unbiased*

Supporting Detail 2: *shows an overall understanding of the course information*

▷ **Coursework**

Supporting Detail 1: *is not good at taking tests – gets nervous*

Supporting Detail 2: *is more room for error*

### ◊ Comparing p.40

**Sample Response 1** Examinations 02-09

The best way to assess a student, in my opinion, is to give examinations. To start, I think that examinations are an unbiased and fair way for teachers to assess students. Let's say a teacher personally dislikes a student. This could be reflected in the way the teacher grades various course assignments. Next, I think that examinations provide a cumulative look at how well a student has absorbed the material in a given semester. The coursework is designed to help the student master tiny portions of the work one piece at a time, but it is only on examinations that the students have the chance to demonstrate that they can put the information together and understand the bigger picture.

**Sample Response 2** Coursework 02-10

To me, it seems that the best way to assess a student is through coursework. The first reason I have for holding this opinion is that not everyone is good at taking tests. Personally, I get nervous on tests and score lower than I should because of that. Even though I get A's on my coursework, I have trouble getting A's on tests because of my nerves. The second reason for my opinion is that coursework gives students more room for error. If you

have a bad day while doing coursework, this is only part of the total assessment, but if you have a bad day during an examination, the effect on your final grade will be much more significant.

---

Chapter **02** | Integrated Speaking

## Task 2 | Emergency-Help Buttons

### Sample Response p.41

**Analyzing**

The announcement is about some emergency kiosks that will be placed around the campus for the students' safety. Students can press the button at the kiosk and get help from campus police within two minutes. The woman is not in favor of the emergency kiosks. She begins by saying that the kiosks will reduce her comfort level on campus. The kiosks give her the impression that the campus isn't safe. She begins to wonder if the university is in a dangerous area, and she claims that the kiosks may make her become paranoid. She also feels that a two-minute response time is not fast enough during an actual emergency. The man compares this response time to response times off campus, but she insists that if she is being mugged or attacked, she won't have time to stand around for two minutes waiting on the police to arrive.

**Deducing**

**Reading**
Topic: *emergency-help kiosks*

**Listening**
Speaker's Opinion: *The woman doesn't like them.*

Reason 1: *make her feel less safe*

Reason 2: *are not effective against street crime*

### ◊ Reading p.42

(Checking)

1 The kiosks are metal boxes with a button and a large red flag on a 10-foot pole.

2 The kiosks will be located around campus along the sidewalks and in front of various buildings.

3 Students can press the button at the kiosk, which alerts patrolling police. The response time is estimated at two minutes.

4 **Critical Thinking:** The kiosks could feature a loud siren that might potentially scare off attackers.

| | |
|---|---|
| **W:** | Whoa. Emergency-help buttons? I didn't realize the campus was so dangerous. |
| **M:** | Maybe the school is installing them just to give an added feeling of safety. |
| **W:** | They don't make me feel any safer. Anyway, the university isn't in a dangerous area, is it? |
| **M:** | Nope. The crime rate is relatively low here. |
| **W:** | That's what I mean. I think these buttons are just going to make me feel paranoid. Now I'll be looking over my shoulder everywhere I go. |
| **M:** | Don't think of them like that. Just know they are there in case of an emergency. Hence the name emergency-help button. |
| **W:** | Say that I do have an emergency. What good would they do? A two-minute response time is too slow. |
| **M:** | That's much faster than emergency services off campus would respond. |
| **W:** | I guess, but how long does it take for someone to mug me or attack me? Maybe ten seconds? Less? |
| **M:** | That's a good point. Well, chances are you'll never need to use one of them anyway. Just don't worry about it. |

### ◊ Planning
p.43

**Her Opinion:** *She does not like the idea of the kiosks.*

Reason 1: *feels less safe because of the kiosks*

Reason 2: *thinks the kiosks are not actually helpful*

Chapter 02 | Integrated Speaking

## Task 3 | Animal Science: Scavenging

### Sample Response
p.44
**Analyzing**

The reading introduces the concept of scavengers as animals that eat the corpses of prey that were killed by other predators. It also says that some scavengers hunt if necessary. The professor elaborates on the concept of scavenger animals by giving examples of scavengers that don't hunt and those that do. She begins with the vulture. The vulture, according the professor, circles overhead sick or dying animals and finishes them off if necessary, but it will not hunt down healthy prey like normal predators do. She then moves on to explain that some scavengers actually hunt down animals. The example she gives is

the hyena. While hyenas prefer to wait for lions or other animals to kill animals and to have their fill, they are no strangers to the hunt. They hunt down and completely devour animals if there are no carcasses available for them to scavenge.

**Deducing**

**Reading**
Topic: *scavenger animals*

**Listening**
Main Idea: *Scavengers usually eat corpses but some hunt.*
Supporting Detail 1: *vultures do not hunt*
Supporting Detail 2: *hyenas sometimes hunt*

### ◊ Reading
p.45
**Checking**

1 Most carnivores are predators and hunt prey for food, but scavengers eat animals that are already dead.

2 Scavengers rely on the work of outside forces to kill their food.

3 Some scavengers only eat carcasses, but others hunt if necessary.

4 **Critical Thinking:** Some scavengers may have better natural offensive traits, such as sharp teeth and claws or fast running speed, which makes them better at hunting.

### ◊ Listening
p.45
Script 02-14

**Professor:** We've all seen the movies and the cartoons that show a vulture circling around over a character to show that the character is near death. Vultures are perhaps the most widely recognized scavenger, and they represent a typical scavenger. In other words, they usually just wait for animals to die before eating them. Sure, they may finish off a wounded or sick animal that's on its way out anyway, but by and large, they tend to wait for other animals or Mother Nature to do the heavy lifting. You won't ever see a vulture hunting down healthy prey the way a typical predator does.

But there are some scavengers that take a more proactive approach to finding food. Take hyenas. Sure, they're scavengers and gladly step in to finish off a devoured carcass after a lion has had its fill, but they are no strangers to the hunt. In fact, they are quite skillful hunters and extremely vicious fighters. Like other large predators, they chase down their target until they are able to catch it by the leg or stomach, after which the pack of hyenas surrounds the animal and rapidly consumes its entire body.

## ◊ Planning p.46

**Main Idea:** *scavengers – some hunt, but most don't*

Supporting Detail 1: *vultures do not hunt; may kill sick animals*

Supporting Detail 2: *hyenas scavenge but do hunt*

---

Chapter **02** | Integrated Speaking

## Task 4 | Astronomy: Ultra-Massive Stars

### Sample Response p.47

**Analyzing**

The professor describes what happens when an ultra-massive star dies. Ultra-massive stars, which have a solar mass of at least 1.4, first go through a supernova phase. This begins when their outer shells very quickly collapse upon their cores because they have run out of energy. The resulting explosion sends atmospheric material flying through space. As this happens, the explosion creates an extremely bright light, which can sometimes be brighter than any other star in its galaxy. Next, depending on its mass, the star can do one of two things. If the star's solar mass is under five, then it becomes a neutron star. Neutron stars have a very high escape velocity that is one-third the speed of light. If the collapsed star's solar mass is over five, then it becomes a black hole, which has no escape velocity because of its extreme gravitational pull and density.

**Deducing**

Topic: *how ultra-massive stars die*

Main Idea: *Ultra-massive stars all explode and become neutron stars or black holes.*

Supporting Detail 1: *neutron star – 1.4 to five solar mass; high escape velocity*

Supporting Detail 2: *black hole – a solar mass over five; no escape velocity*

## ◊ Listening p.48

Script 02-16

**Professor:** So we talked on Tuesday about white dwarfs, which ninety-seven percent of all stars become when they die. But it's important to understand what can happen to ultra-massive stars, or those with a solar mass of at least 1.4. There are basically two possible eventual outcomes for large stars depending on their mass, but all of them first undergo the supernova process.

As we discussed last time, a star dies when it runs out of energy and the outer shell collapses in on the core. For ultra-massive stars, this rapid collapse—which takes only fifteen seconds to complete—causes an explosion that sends the star's atmospheric layers flying through space. The supernova explosion creates a light so bright that we can sometimes see it with our naked eye from Earth. The explosion is so bright, actually, that it can outshine any other star in its galaxy. After the explosion, the mass of the star is dramatically reduced, and all that's left are the core elements, such as iron.

What happens next depends on the mass of the star's remnants. If the solar mass is 1.4 to five, then it becomes a neutron star. Neutron stars have an incredible gravitational pull due to their extreme density. The escape velocity, or speed required for matter to leave a neutron star, is about 100,000 kilometers per second. That's one-third the speed of light. So what happens when a star's remnants are more than five solar masses? Well, then you get a black hole. As you are probably aware, a black hole's gravitational pull is so strong that there is no escape velocity; matter simply cannot escape.

## ◊ Planning p.48

**Main Idea:** *Ultra-massive stars die in the same way but can become two things.*

Supporting Detail 1: *smaller stars become neutron stars – 1/3 c (speed of light) escape velocity*

Supporting Detail 2: *larger stars become black holes – no escape velocity*

## Task 1 | Career: Money or Enjoyment

### ◈ Planning
p.50

▷ **Salary > Enjoyment**

Supporting Detail 1: *live a life of luxury*

Supporting Detail 2: *become a philanthropist*

▷ **Enjoyment > Salary**

Supporting Detail 1: *less stress; healthier life*

Supporting Detail 2: *cannot excel at a job you dislike*

### ◈ Comparing
p.50

**Sample Response 1**  Salary > Enjoyment  **02-17**

I would prefer to have a job that earns a higher salary over a job that I enjoy. The first reason for my preference is that I hope one day to live a life of luxury. I see celebrities and others on TV who are able to travel in limousines and private jets. One day, I would like to live that kind of lifestyle, and having a job that commands a high salary would allow me to do that. The next reason is that I would like to become a philanthropist one day. I've been inspired by people such as Bill Gates, who gives billions of dollars to help people in need. My dream is one day to be able to earn enough money that I could help people in significant ways.

**Sample Response 2**  Enjoyment > Salary  **02-18**

I would prefer to have a job that I enjoy even if it doesn't pay a very high salary. For one thing, I believe that having a job I enjoy would allow me to live a less stressful life. In today's world, many people are stressed out because they are overworked in jobs they don't enjoy. If I could build a career doing work that I truly enjoy, then I would experience less stress and therefore live a longer, healthier life. Not only that, but I also believe you cannot truly do a job well unless you enjoy it. If I chose a career I didn't enjoy, I wouldn't be able to excel in that career. But if I had a career that I was passionate about, I could become a leading expert in my field.

## Task 2 | Road Closure

### Sample Response
p.51

**Analyzing**

The man and the woman are having a conversation about the school's decision to close Martinson Road to all vehicular traffic. From now on, only pedestrians will be allowed on the road. The reason given for this change is that there have been too many accidents involving vehicles and pedestrians on the road. The woman has mixed feelings about the decision by the university. On the one hand, she understands the decision because too many people have gotten hurt lately. She states that there have been five accidents on the road in just one month. One of the people who was injured in an accident there is her friend, who is still in the hospital. On the other hand, she comments that she dislikes group punishment. She explains that every driver is being punished by the actions of a few irresponsible drivers. In that regard, she dislikes the way that the school is handling the situation.

**Deducing**

**Reading**

Topic: *Martinson Road is being closed to all vehicles.*

**Listening**

Speaker's opinion: *The woman has mixed feelings about it.*

Reason 1: *are too many accidents on the road*

Reason 2: *does not think good drivers should be punished because of bad drivers*

### ◈ Reading
p.52

**Checking**

1   It is closing the road to all traffic, including cars, trucks, vans, motorbikes, and bicycles.

2   There have been several accidents involving vehicles and pedestrians on the road recently.

3   The school hopes that students will be able safely to walk to their classes and other destinations.

4   **Critical Thinking:** The school could have more traffic police to make sure that vehicles are driving safely, and it could also ensure that vehicles do not speed on the road.

## Listening

p.52

Script 02-20

M: I can't believe it. How am I supposed to go to my classes if I can't drive on Martinson Road anymore?

W: You know, I understand why the school has made this decision. There have been five accidents on that road this semester, and it has barely been a month since winter break ended.

M: But those students were in the road where they didn't belong.

W: True, but drivers have to be more responsible. One of my friends got hit by a car there, and she's still in the hospital.

M: So you totally support this decision by the school?

W: Not at all. I understand the reasoning behind it, but I also dislike the decision.

M: How so?

W: Well, you're right. Now, students like you are going to have to take major detours to drive to your classes. That's a huge inconvenience. So safe drivers are being punished for the actions of a few bad drivers. That's group punishment, which is something I don't support.

## Planning

p.53

**Her Opinion:** *She has mixed feelings about the decision.*

Reason 1: *thinks there are too many accidents*

Reason 2: *does not support group punishment*

---

Chapter 03 | Integrated Speaking

## Task 3 | Natural Science: Bioluminescence

### Sample Response

p.54

Analyzing

Bioluminescence is the ability of plants and animals to produce light naturally. The light is used for a number of different reasons. The professor begins by giving examples of sea creatures that produce light in the deep sea. The first that he mentions is the anglerfish, which has an appendage coming out from its head which the fish uses to attract prey. The professor also mentions crustaceans, which use light to attract potential mates. The professor then moves on to give examples of land-dwelling organisms that produce light. The first example of fireflies illustrates again the ability of creatures to use bioluminescence to attract mates. In addition to fireflies,

---

there are also glowing mushrooms in the forest. Their light is possibly used to signal to predators that the mushrooms are toxic, but scientists are unsure of exactly what purpose the light serves.

Deducing

**Reading**

Topic: *bioluminescence*

**Listening**

Main Idea: *used for various purposes*

Supporting Detail 1: *deep-sea creatures that attract prey and mates*

Supporting Detail 2: *land organisms that attract mates; deter predators*

## Reading

p.55

Checking

1 Bioluminescence is a light that is a byproduct of chemical reactions in living organisms.

2 The light is usually blue or green, but sometimes it is red or yellow.

3 The light can be used to attract mates or prey, to camouflage the organism, and possibly to communicate with and scare off attackers.

4 **Critical Thinking:** Some animals might grow very large eyes. Plants may adapt by using something besides sunlight to do photosynthesis.

## Listening

p.55

Script 02-22

Professor: Imagine being in the deep sea some 2,000 meters below the surface of the water. At that depth in the ocean, the water column has completely filtered out all light from the sun. What would you see? Nothing? Actually, the deep sea is alive with light. It's estimated that some ninety percent of deep-sea creatures produce light by a process called bioluminescence.

One of the more well-known instances of this is the anglerfish. This ugly little creature has an appendage that sticks out from its head and hangs in front of its face. At the end of the appendage is a glowing lure that attracts smaller fish directly into the anglerfish's open mouth. Certain species of crustaceans also use coded light signals to attract mates during mating season.

Now, the deep sea isn't the only place where you'll find bioluminescent organisms. Can you think of a flying insect that emits a soft greenish glow? That's right. It's the firefly. It uses its light to attract mates, to communicate its location to other fireflies, and to, ah . . . to repel predators from larva.

But it is not only animals that can glow in the dark. Some mushrooms have the ability to create bioluminescent light, which is typically emitted through the bottom of the mushroom cap. Scientists don't know the exact reason for this ability in mushrooms, but it's speculated that the light serves as a warning that the mushrooms are toxic and thus unsafe to eat.

### ◊ Planning

**Main Idea:** *Bioluminescence is light produced by organisms in the deep sea and forests for various reasons.*

Supporting Detail 1: *deep sea – used to attract prey and mates*

Supporting Detail 2: *forest – attract mates; deter predators*

---

Chapter **03** | Integrated Speaking

### Task 4 | Sociology: Social Construction

### Sample Response

p.57

**Analyzing**

The professor uses a news story to explain the concept of social construction, which means that we each have a subjective perception of reality. The professor begins the lecture with a story which is about an African-American Harvard professor who is arrested at his own home. The police officer in the story is Caucasian, and he arrests the professor, who appeared to have been breaking into his own home. The two men in the story interpreted the event very differently—one as a racist act and the other as a simple police procedure. The professor then explains that this story illustrates social construction. This is the idea there is no true objective reality and that instead we each understand the world based on our own experiences and knowledge. As illustrated in the example of the Harvard professor and the police officer, social construction can create problems in our everyday lives due to misunderstandings.

**Deducing**

Topic: *social construction*

Main Idea: *Reality is not objective; it is subjective due to perceptions.*

Supporting Detail 1: *story of Harvard professor and police officer*

Supporting Detail 2: *social construction of reality – meaning is created by personal experience*

### ◊ Listening

p.58

Script 02-24

**Professor:** Let's talk today a bit about how we each perceive the world. Consider the following real scenario that takes place in Boston. A Harvard professor arrives at his home late one night after a long flight. His door is jammed, and he has to ram it with his shoulder a few times to get it open. A woman across the street, thinking she is witnessing a burglary, calls the police. A police sergeant arrives and demands to see the professor's ID. The professor, an African-American, insists the Caucasian officer has no right to ask for ID and calls the officer a racist. Angry words are exchanged, and the professor is arrested. What we have here are two very different views of the same event. The professor, as I said, feels the cop is requesting ID only because of his skin color while the cop feels that he is just doing his job by protecting a homeowner and by following procedure for responding to a break-in call.

How can this happen? Why can't both men view the situation through the same lens? This happens because of what we call social construction, a facet of the human mind that shapes every part of our social lives. The basic concept here is that there is really no such thing as an objective reality. We as humans have certain beliefs and expectations about everyone else in society, and we interpret situations in terms of those beliefs. So in the example of the Boston cop and the Harvard professor, each person acted based on his own subjective construction of reality. As you can see, social construction can lead to a lot of problems due to genuine misunderstandings.

### ◊ Planning

p.58

**Main Idea:** *social construction = no objective reality*

Supporting Detail 1: *story of Harvard professor and police officer*

Supporting Detail 2: *definition: no objective reality due to personal perceptions*

## Task 1 | **Teaching Formally vs. Teaching Casually**

### ◈ Planning                                    p.60

▷ **Teach Formally**

Advantages: *better classroom discipline; students pay attention and learn more*

Disadvantages: *can be boring; some students don't like*

▷ **Teach Casually**

Advantages: *more fun for students; can relate to students better*

Disadvantages: *students learn less; students don't always respect teacher*

### ◈ Comparing                                    p.60

**Sample Response 1**  Teach Formally                    02-25

There are both advantages and disadvantages to instructors teaching formally. Regarding some advantages, first of all, formal instructors often have better classroom discipline because their students do not misbehave. Students also tend to pay more attention in formal classes, so they learn more as a result. This helps students improve their overall knowledge of various subjects. However, there are also disadvantages to this teaching method. One of the drawbacks is that instructors who teach formally can often be boring. The reason is that they normally simply stand up in front of the class and deliver their lectures. In addition, some students don't like these types of classes, so they don't enjoy their time in them. This can cause some students not to learn as much as they should in formal classes.

**Sample Response 2**  Teach Casually                    02-26

I can think of quite a few advantages and disadvantages of having instructors who teach casually. First of all, one advantage is that students in these classes frequently have more fun. Casual instructors have a tendency to be more entertaining, so students enjoy these classes. These instructors are also better able to relate to their students, so students may open up and be more willing to participate in class discussions. On the negative side, students in classes with casual instructors sometimes

don't learn as much as they should. They are so focused on having fun that they may forget to learn the material. Some students also have less respect for their instructors. For instance, they might call their instructors by their first names and not always behave properly in class.

## Task 2 | **New Internet-Based Courses**

### Sample Response                                p.61

**Analyzing**

The students are discussing an announcement about new online courses being offered at the university. At first, the woman is interested in the online courses, but after some discussion, she decides that she is not a good candidate for them. Her first reason for her opinion is that she feels she is a brick-and-mortar type of person. This means that she enjoys being in a physical location to take a class more than she would enjoy studying online. The man says the Internet is the way of the future, but she says that she likes to discuss topics with other students and the professor in the classroom so that she can better understand the material. She also states that she doesn't think she is self-motivated enough to complete an online course. She worries that she will procrastinate and not get her coursework completed on time.

**Deducing**

**Reading**

Topic: *Online courses are now offered.*

**Listening**

Speaker's Opinion: *The woman will not sign up.*

Reason 1: *prefers to be in a physical classroom*

Reason 2: *thinks she will procrastinate*

### ◈ Reading                                    p.62

**Checking**

1   The new program is a selection of courses offered online.

2   Students participate by using textbooks at home and possibly by watching live lectures on a secure server.

3   Students who wish to sign up should speak with their academic advisors and purchase the necessary materials.

4   **Critical Thinking:** Commuting students are given

priority because they would benefit the most from online courses since they have to drive to the university otherwise.

## ◈ Listening

p.62

Script 02-28

M: Check this out, Angie. Looks like good news for you, huh?

W: Online courses? It's something to think about, for sure.

M: I thought you'd be excited about it. You commute forty-five minutes each way, right?

W: Yes, that's true. I'm not so happy about buying gas and putting so many miles on my car, but honestly, I'm more of a brick-and-mortar kind of person.

M: That's so outdated. The Internet is the future of education. What can you get by driving to class that you can't get from an online course?

W: For one thing, I enjoy the banter between the professor and the students. Do you know what I mean?

M: I'm not sure I follow.

W: Well, students can ask questions, and my professors often elicit opinions from students to get conversations going. This really helps me absorb the material better.

M: Okay, but with online courses, they have discussion boards where people can post questions.

W: Mm-hmm . . . It's not really the same though. But then there's the question of motivation. If I don't have a routine schedule, I know I'll procrastinate with my studies.

M: That's true. You do need to be self-motivated to do online courses.

## ◈ Planning

p.63

**Her Opinion:** *She does not want to sign up for online courses.*

Reason 1: *prefers physical classrooms*

Reason 2: *is not self-motivated enough*

## Task 3 | Philosophy: Transcendentalism

### Sample Response

p.64

Analyzing

The Transcendentalists were thinkers in the early nineteenth century who opposed the popular thought of their day and developed a philosophy from their discontent. At that time in New England, the dominant religious group was the Unitarians. They did not believe in strictly following church doctrine or biblical interpretations. Instead, they believed that people should use rational thought in order to understand the divine. In contrast, the Transcendentalists felt that the divine was everywhere around them and was one and the same with nature. They said that people cannot understand the divine without feeling nature. Thus, they opposed the "corpse cold" Unitarian group and began their new philosophy, which emphasized learning to appreciate nature as a way to see God. So Transcendentalism came not only from a love of nature and the desire to see the divine through it but also from a resistance to contemporary religious philosophy.

Deducing

**Reading**

Topic: *Transcendentalism*

**Listening**

Main Idea: *began out of opposition to major ideas of the day*

Supporting Detail 1: *contemporary thinkers, Unitarians: rational thought to see the divine*

Supporting Detail 2: *Transcendentalists: used feelings and emotion about nature to see the divine*

## ◈ Reading

p.65

Checking

1   The goal of Transcendentalism was to deliver speeches and to write essays about a new philosophy.

2   They believed that one should use one's senses rather than rational thought to understand the divine.

3   One must first understand the religious context of the day before one can understand Transcendentalism.

4   **Critical Thinking:** They must have been people who loved nature and who had a great passion for life.

Script 02-30

**Professor:** When we think of Thoreau or Emerson today, we might be quick to assume they were, ah . . . nature lovers, a sort of nineteenth-century precursor to the hippies of the 1960s. It is true that they strongly emphasized nature, but we really have to look at Transcendentalism's roots to get an idea of why.

During the last half of the eighteenth century, a Christian denomination known as Unitarianism became the dominant religion in the Boston area. The Unitarians were a unique bunch in terms of their approach to Christianity. Unlike the Calvinists and other orthodox sects, Unitarians did not believe in following strict church doctrine or biblical interpretation. Rather, they promoted rational thought as a way to determine ethical conduct and to understand the Bible.

The young thinkers who were to become the Transcendentalists felt that Unitarianism was, in the words of Emerson, "corpse cold." It lacked a spiritual quality that they desired. This brings us to their conception of nature: The Transcendentalists believed that the divine was everywhere at once and that God, in fact, was nature. Strictly rational thought, they believed, was not enough. Instead, they stressed being close to nature so that one might "feel" the presence of God. As you can imagine, this caused quite a stir in the religious and academic communities of their day.

◈ **Planning**      p.66

**Main Idea:** *Transcendentalism arose as a rejection of contemporary religious thought.*

Supporting Detail 1: *religious context: Unitarians, rational thought*

Supporting Detail 2: *Transcendentalists: nature, feeling*

Chapter **04** | Integrated Speaking

Task **4** | **Business: Job Sharing**

## Sample Response
p.67

**Analyzing**

The professor lectures on job sharing. She defines it as a situation in which two or more people do the work that one person would normally do. She remarks that job sharers split the hours and the salary for their position. Job sharing is something parents with children like since they want to work yet also be with their children. The professor

discusses two disadvantages of job sharing. The first is that job sharers may have different approaches to their jobs. She uses the example of two elementary school teachers splitting teaching duties. If one is strict while the other is not, then the students might become confused and not learn well. The second disadvantage she mentions is that there are often lots of communication errors. Colleagues need to keep the job sharers updated, but they might forget to do that at times. As a result, mistakes such as missed meetings or work that doesn't get done could happen.

**Deducing**

Topic: *job sharing*

Main Idea: *There are disadvantages to two or more workers doing the job of one full-time employee.*

Supporting Detail 1: *different job approaches can be confusing*

Supporting Detail 2: *are often many communication errors*

◈ **Listening**      p.68

Script 02-32

**Professor:** In recent years, job sharing has been increasing in popularity. In case you haven't heard of it, basically, job sharing is an arrangement in which two or more individuals share the work normally done by a single full-time employee. People who do job sharing therefore work reduced hours and split the pay. It's especially popular with parents who want to take time off to be with their children but still want to work.

I can see the appeal of job sharing, yet there are also disadvantages to this arrangement that you should be aware of. For instance, most people don't have the same approach to their job that others do. Let's think about a job-sharing arrangement at an elementary school. Perhaps one person teaches a class in the morning while another person comes in after lunch to teach in the afternoon. Now, the morning teacher might be very strict and doesn't let the students ask questions. But the afternoon teacher prefers that the students have class discussions and lets them play around. Those are two very different teaching styles, and that can confuse students and make it difficult for them to learn.

Another disadvantage is that when there is job sharing, communication errors often proliferate. Think about an office job covered by one person three days a week and another two days a week. These two workers' colleagues have to keep both of them updated about what's going on in the office. But what happens if someone forgets to inform one of the workers about a key meeting or an important project? In that case, a meeting might not be attended, or some work might not get done. That could cause problems for the job sharers' colleagues. And that's why I'm strongly against job sharing.

### ◈ Planning

p.68

**Main Idea:** *Job sharing has some disadvantages.*

Supporting Detail 1: *can confuse students*

Supporting Detail 2: *communication errors proliferate*

---

**Chapter 05 | Independent Speaking**

## Task 1 | Living Alone vs. Roommates

### ◈ Planning

p.70

▷ **Live Alone**

Supporting Detail 1: *greater privacy – showers; waking up; no forced conversations*

Supporting Detail 2: *meet more people – must join student activities and meet new friends*

▷ **Have Roommates**

Supporting Detail 1: *social person – someone to talk to and eat and watch TV with*

Supporting Detail 2: *easier household maintenance – share responsibilities for cooking & cleaning*

### ◈ Comparing

p.70

**Sample Response 1** Live Alone          02-33

I'd prefer to live alone when I go to university. Above all, I am a very private person. I like to know that when I'm sleeping, showering, or doing anything else, I won't have someone to worry about. Along these same lines, when I wake up in the morning or come home tired from class or work, I won't have to put on a smile and make conversation with anyone. Equally important is that not having roommates would force me to get out of the house and meet many people. If I had roommates, I might be tempted to sit around watching TV or playing video games with them, but if I lived alone, I'd have to join student clubs or participate in other activities outside of the home, which would help me meet a greater variety of people.

**Sample Response 2** Have Roommates          02-34

I can't imagine living alone. I would have to live with roommates if I moved away to attend university. For starters, I'm a very social person. I love to have people around and cannot stand a quiet house. I like to have someone to talk to when I get home from class or to eat dinner and watch TV with. It would be very lonely living alone. In addition to that, I think living with a roommate would help me to prepare with working in an office in the future. It's important for office workers to get along and peacefully to resolve conflicts. Sharing a small dorm room with someone for four years would certainly give me plenty of opportunities to hone my people skills.

---

**Chapter 05 | Integrated Speaking**

## Task 2 | Library Renovations

### Sample Response

p.71

**Analyzing**

The two students are talking about the library being closed for renovations. The man is excited about the announcement because the renovations will improve the library in a couple of ways that will benefit him. The first thing that he mentions is that the computer lab will be improved. He says that he does not have a computer at home, so he does most of his computer-based research from on-campus computer labs. After the renovations, the computers in the library will access the database more quickly and facilitate his research. He also says that he is happy about the increased number of study rooms that will be added. Students currently must put their names on waiting lists in order to access study rooms. The man expects that, after the renovations, there will be plenty of rooms available, so waiting lists won't be needed.

**Deducing**

**Reading**

Topic: *The library is partially closing for renovations.*

**Listening**

Speaker's Opinion: *The man is happy about the renovations.*

Reason 1: *better computer lab*

Reason 2: *more study rooms*

## ◊ Reading

p.72

**Checking**

1    The announcement publicizes the renovation schedule of the library primarily to let students know that library access will be limited for several months.

2    The computer lab will be improved, more reference materials and study rooms will be added, and the décor will be more comfortable.

3    Students will only be able to access the reference materials during construction.

4    **Critical Thinking:** Students might be upset about the partial closing of the library during the beginning part of the semester or during summer school.

## ◊ Listening

p.72

Script 02-36

W:  Aw, this is just great. For the first two months of next semester, we'll essentially have no library.

M:  I think it'll be worth the wait. Imagine how nice the new computer lab will be. You know how the computers in all the computer labs are as slow as molasses? This will really help with our database research.

W:  I'm just as happy to do my research from home.

M:  Well, I don't have a home computer, so I always use the labs on campus. It'll be nice to have one with up-to-date computers.

W:  Yeah . . . but, you know, I use the library a lot for study groups and when we have group projects in class.

M:  See? There's something for everyone.

W:  No, what I mean is that with the library closed for basically half the semester, I won't have anywhere to meet.

M:  You can meet somewhere else on campus. Just think: Once the renovations are done, it'll be easier for you to get a study room here. There will be no more putting your name on waiting lists to get a room for your group.

W:  I just wish the library didn't have to close down for so long.

## ◊ Planning

p.73

**His Opinion:** *He is happy about the renovations.*

Reason 1: *will be a better computer lab*

Reason 2: *will be more study rooms*

---

## Task 3 | Medicine: Penicillin

### Sample Response

p.74

**Analyzing**

Penicillin was accidentally discovered by Alexander Fleming when he saw mold growing in a Petri dish he had left uncovered. The mold stopped infectious bacteria from spreading. This, the reading claims, changed the world. This argument is supported by the lecture. The professor begins the lecture by arguing that the advent of widespread penicillin use was the most important medical advancement in history. He says that before penicillin came into popular use, people usually became crippled or died from most infections. Penicillin also led the way to antibiotics becoming commonplace, which further improved public health. Another global impact of penicillin is on world population. The professor explains that the world's population would be about half of what it is today if not for penicillin. The reason is that many of our grandparents would have died from infections as children or as a result of wounds received in battle during wars.

**Deducing**

**Reading**

Topic: *penicillin*

**Listening**

Main Idea: *most important medicine: penicillin*

Supporting Detail 1: *protected many people from dying of infections*

Supporting Detail 2: *responsible for world population – many would have died from infections*

## ◊ Reading

p.75

**Checking**

1    He left a Petri dish uncovered, and it started growing mold.

2    It stopped the spread of infectious bacteria.

3    Medicine was revolutionized, and the world was changed.

4    **Critical Thinking:** Birth rates would be higher because the infant mortality rate would still be high.

Professor: Someone once asked me what I thought the most important medicine ever made is. It was an easy question to answer, really, and I'm sure you all know what I said: penicillin. Before penicillin was finalized as a viable, mass-produced medicine sometime in the thirties, there was very little doctors could do if someone got a serious bacterial infection. In most cases, patients either died or were left severely crippled. With penicillin, doctors learned that antibiotic agents could fight the bacteria and stop the spread of infections. Today, antibiotics are so common in medicine that we don't even think about them, but fewer than 100 years ago, they didn't exist at all.

So you can see that penicillin had a profound effect on the world. No longer did children who got serious infections die. With a much-reduced infant mortality rate, that means there soon were more people on the Earth. And these people then had children. Some say the world's population would be half of what it is today without penicillin as most of our grandparents would have succumbed to illnesses before reaching adulthood. Think of the millions of wounded soldiers in World War II alone who would have died from infections had they not been treated with penicillin. Many of us in this classroom may never have been born without penicillin.

◈ **Planning**        p.76

**Main Idea:** *Penicillin was the most important medical advancement ever.*

Supporting Detail 1: *changed medicine – people no longer died from infections*

Supporting Detail 2: *the world's population is double what it would have been without penicillin*

Chapter **05** | Integrated Speaking

## Task 4 | Engineering: Arches

**Sample Response**      p.77

Analyzing

According to the professor, innovations in engineering can alter the course of history. He makes this point by talking about how the Romans used arches to expand their empire. One of the ways they used arches was in the construction of bridges. Since the Roman Empire was spread all across Europe, there was very much terrain that needed to be crossed by the army. The arch allowed the Romans to create sturdy bridges, which in turn allowed the army to quickly travel to any location in Europe that needed immediate military attention. The other way the Romans spread their empire by using arches was with aqueducts. Arches allowed the construction of aqueducts to carry water to conquered people. Because providing water to ordinary people was unheard of at the time, the people became loyal to the Roman Empire. So by providing quick mobilization and gaining people's loyalty, arches helped the spread of the Roman Empire.

Deducing

Topic: *arches used in engineering*

Main Idea: *used to spread the Roman Empire*

Supporting Detail 1: *allowed the quick mobilization of army with bridges*

Supporting Detail 2: *won the loyalty of conquered people with aqueducts*

◈ **Listening**         p.78

Script 02-40

Professor: While we're on the subject of Roman architecture, I'd like to take a moment to tell you about how seemingly simple engineering innovations can change the course of history. As you've seen, the arch was a key component of Roman architecture. Now, they didn't invent the arch, but they were the first to put it to good use, and it ended up playing a major part in the expansion of the Roman Empire.

One of the primary concerns for any army is transportation. Recall that the Roman Empire stretched all the way from Persia to Britain. That's a lot of land to cover. So how did the arch assist in the quick mobilization of Roman forces when they were needed? Bridges. Roman bridges, which heavily involved arches in their design, were amazingly sturdy. They consisted of a road built atop a series of adjacent arches. Since arches are used to distribute weight evenly across structures, these bridges were in no danger of collapsing. Even better, if one part of a bridge happened to be damaged or destroyed, the entire bridge did not collapse, so only the damaged part needed to be mended before the army could continue its journey.

Another concern of the empire was ensuring the loyalty of the people in the lands it had conquered. Arches again came to the rescue by allowing the construction of elaborate aqueducts. Like bridges, aqueducts were built using successive arches. The strength of this design provided a reliable way to deliver clean water to people throughout the Roman Empire. The idea that ordinary people were provided with drinking and bathing water by Rome made quite an impression on conquered people and easily won the loyalty of a good many of them.

## ◐ Planning                                                      p.78

**Main Idea:** *Arches helped spread the Roman Empire.*

Supporting Detail 1: *bridges allowed the quick mobilization of the army*

Supporting Detail 2: *aqueducts made conquered people loyal*

---

**Chapter 06 | Independent Speaking**

## Task 1 | How to Use a New Piece of Equipment

### ◐ Planning                                                     p.80

▷ **Consult the User's Manual**

Supporting Detail 1: *find out exactly what to do*
Supporting Detail 2: *learn how to avoid dangerous problems*

▷ **Ask Another Person for Assistance**

Supporting Detail 1: *learn from someone with experience*
Supporting Detail 2: *find out important information not in the user's manual*

### ◐ Comparing                                                    p.80

**Sample Response 1** Consult the User's Manual        02-41

Of the three choices, I would opt to consult the user's manual. One reason is that the user's manual will explain exactly what to do. Recently, my family purchased a washing machine. My parents read the user's manual to learn how to operate it. Because they did that, they haven't had any problems with it. Another reason to consult the user's manual is that you can learn how to avoid dangerous problems. For instance, I read the user's manual for my family's microwave oven. I'm glad I did because I learned not to put metal in a microwave. It could change the taste of the food, burn the food, or even cause a fire. If I hadn't read the user's manual, I might have done something dangerous.

**Sample Response 2** Ask Another Person for Assistance   02-42

Each choice is good, but the best is to ask another person for assistance. The primary reason is that I can learn from someone with experience. I used an electric drill for my science project last month. I asked my father for help. He explained precisely how to use the drill. As a result, my science project looked great, and I learned to use a new piece of equipment. A secondary reason is that I can find out important information not in the user's manual. My father gave me some tips while using the drill. He told me it can start shaking at times, so I was ready when that happened. I might have dropped the drill out of surprise if I hadn't known what to expect.

---

**Chapter 06 | Integrated Speaking**

## Task 2 | New Dormitory Opening

### Sample Response                                                p.81

**Analyzing**

The woman sees the announcement about the new, high-quality dormitory on campus but decides that she does not want to live there. Her first reason for having that opinion is that she thinks the dorm is too expensive. At 14,000 dollars a year, it is almost 6,000 dollars more expensive than the other dorms. Instead, she prefers to find an apartment off campus, which she thinks will cost much less overall, even after she considers the cost of rent and groceries. She also says that she does not wish to follow the rules of the dormitory. Even though she would like to be on campus to participate in activities and to involve herself in the community, she does not think she can abide the restrictions placed on students in dorms. One of the rules she mentions is the curfew, which she does not want to obey.

**Deducing**

**Reading**
Topic: *new dormitory*

**Listening**
Speaker's Opinion: *is not planning on living there*
Reason 1: *is too expensive*
Reason 2: *dislikes the dormitory rules*

## ◆ Reading    p.82

(Checking)

1   The announcement lets students know about a new dormitory that has been built, most likely in the hope that students will register to live there.

2   The dormitory offers private bathrooms, kitchenettes, group study rooms, laundry facilities, and a common area with a TV.

3   Students receive free access to the laundry facilities and a meal plan as part of the cost of living in the dormitory.

4   **Critical Thinking:** Students living off campus have more freedoms and probably pay lower rent but are farther from the university and thus are less likely to participate in campus activities.

## ◆ Listening    p.82

Script 02-44

M: I know where I'm living when we get to college this fall. What a dorm! Are you going to sign up for a room there, too?

W: Fourteen-thousand dollars a year? For a dorm? What a rip-off. The other dorms on campus are only eighty-five hundred.

M: And they're nowhere nearly as good. Think about the convenience of a laundry facility right on your floor. And the privacy of your own room and bathroom, not to mention the meal plan.

W: I was thinking about renting an apartment off campus. Rent is around 500 dollars a month, and groceries would only be about 300 dollars. I could save a lot of money that way.

M: Maybe it's a little cheaper, but don't you want to be involved with the school community? Commuters just don't have the same college experience.

W: I'll get involved with clubs and activities, but honestly, I wouldn't want to live in a dorm at all. Dealing with a curfew and all of the other rules would really annoy me.

M: To each her own, but I still think you'll be missing out.

## ◆ Planning    p.83

**Her Opinion:** *She will not live in the dorm.*

Reason 1: *off-campus living is cheaper*

Reason 2: *doesn't like the dorm rules*

---

## Task 3 | **Psychology: Birth Order**

### Sample Response    p.84

**Analyzing**

The reading explains that birth order is when a person is born relative to his or her siblings, as in first-born, middle, youngest, and so forth. Some psychologists claim that firstborn siblings have attributes of leadership and control while younger-born siblings are less likely to be overachievers and tend to dislike responsibility more. The professor confirms this assertion by presenting examples of sports figures and politicians. She names three first-born successes who are in the top ranks of their field while their younger siblings are much less accomplished. The professor goes on to say that birth order can affect not only people's personalities but also their intelligence. Citing recent research, she says that first-born siblings have an average of 2.3 more IQ points than their next-born siblings and that average IQs become lower as one goes down the birth order. This is attributed to the fact that first-born children must figure out how to do things by themselves and then go on to teach these things to their younger siblings.

**Deducing**

**Reading**

Topic: *birth order and personality*

**Listening**

Main Idea: *Birth order affects personality and intelligence.*

Supporting Detail 1: *athletes and politicians who are first-born overachievers – younger siblings are not as successful*

Supporting Detail 2: *the average IQ is lower in younger siblings*

### ◆ Reading    p.85

(Checking)

1   Birth order is when you were born in relation to your siblings.

2   First-born siblings are more controlling, protective, and authoritarian than their younger siblings.

3   Like children without siblings, the youngest children tend to dislike responsibility and love attention.

4   **Critical Thinking:** In the nature vs. nurture debate, this passage asserts a strong "nature" position as the dominant influence of one's personality.

Professor: Some psychologists claim that birth order can have a profound effect on someone's character attributes throughout that person's life. This phenomenon has been observed in famous siblings who demonstrate the older sibling -younger sibling dynamic quite well. In sports, you have baseball players Dom DiMaggio and Billy Ripken. Both were minor stars and were probably known only because of the fame of their older brothers, whose names I'm sure you know: Joe DiMaggio and Cal Ripken, Jr. In politics, you have Teddy Roosevelt, a stereotypical first-born overachiever, and his younger brother Elliot, who became an alcoholic and drug addict and never achieved much of anything.

But recent research has shown that birth order affects more than personality; it can also affect one's intelligence. That's right, folks. First-born children have an average of 2.3 more IQ points than their next-younger sibling, and the IQ scale gets lower as you go down the birth order. The reason for this actually makes a lot of sense. Older children have to learn all of their cognitive and motor skills pretty much on their own, so they teach themselves. Then, when their kid sister or brother comes along, the older sibling becomes a teacher and reinforces his or her own knowledge through instruction to the younger siblings. This provides a mental jump-start on life for first-borns.

◈ **Planning**     p.86

**Main Idea:** *Birth order has an effect on our personality and intelligence.*

Supporting Detail 1: *examples – sports stars, politicians, and older siblings are more successful than younger siblings*

Supporting Detail 2: *IQ is higher in older siblings*

---

Chapter **06** | Integrated Speaking

Task **4** | **Geology: Glacier Landforms**

**Sample Response**     p.87

Analyzing

The lecture is about how the retreat of glaciers during the last major ice age caused various land formations on the Earth today. The professor begins by explaining how the ice sheet that moved across North America created enormous lakes. The first example given is the Great Lakes, which are located on the border of the United States and Canada. The ice sheet knocked down mountains and made gigantic holes, which were later filled with melted ice. The second example is Lake Agassiz in the middle of Canada. It was formed by an ice sheet pressing down on the land. The professor then moves to some other landforms created by ice. These are the fjords of Norway and Iceland. As the ice retreated, it picked up rocks and pebbles, which gave it strong abrasive power. The ice tore up the land as it moved, creating interesting-looking fjords that we can see on maps today.

Deducing

Topic: *how the ice age changed the shape of the Earth*

Main Idea: *Ice created massive lakes and unusual landforms.*

Supporting Detail 1: *massive lakes: Great Lakes & Lake Agassiz*

Supporting Detail 2: *unusual landforms: the fjords of Norway & Iceland*

◈ **Listening**     p.88

Script 02-48

Professor: During the final advance of the last ice age about 30,000 years ago, an ice sheet that was about a kilometer thick moved across northern North America. It fully retreated 11,000 years ago, but not before leaving indelible marks on the geography of the continent by forming massive lakes and unusual landforms.

If you were to go back two million years and look for the Great Lakes, you wouldn't be able to find them. When the ice sheet advanced across North America, it ripped apart this land by knocking down mountains and by digging out gigantic holes. As the ice retreated, its edges melted and filled those holes with water. What it left behind were these five beautiful lakes that we share with Canada today. But the ice wasn't done there. As it had spent a great deal of time in the mid-regions of Canada, its incredible weight pressed down on the earth there, creating a basin of about 440,000 square kilometers. This created Lake Agassiz, which contained more water than all of the current lakes in the world combined. You may not have heard of this one since it drained out through the St. Lawrence River a few thousand years ago.

But the ice did more than create lakes. As it moved along the ground, it tore apart rocks and carried dirt and pebbles with it. This added to the weight and abrasive power of the ice, which carved some interesting landforms as it swept across continents. For example, the beautiful fjords of Norway and Iceland. The retreating ice sheet and glaciers had such a drastic effect that you can look at a map today and see the coasts of both countries are lined with fjords.

### ◊ Planning
p.88

**Main Idea:** *Retreating glaciers in the last ice age changed the Earth in drastic ways.*

Supporting Detail 1: *created enormous lakes*

Supporting Detail 2: *created fjords*

# Part B-2
## Mastering Knowledge & Skills for the Speaking Test

### Task 1 | **Living on or off Campus**

### ◊ Planning
p.90

**On Campus**

Supporting Detail 1: *don't need a car*

Supporting Detail 2: *save time*

**Off Campus**

Supporting Detail 1: *more privacy*

Supporting Detail 2: *more comfortable*

### ◊ Grading
p.90

**Sample Response 1** On Campus
02-49

I'd prefer to live on campus when I go to university. There are a couple of reasons for my opinion. For one thing, I do not want to own a car when I'm attending university. Since most things that students require are right on campus, I'd never need to have a personal vehicle to go anywhere. Instead, I could just walk, ride my bicycle, or take an on-campus bus. The other reason I'd prefer to live on campus is that I could save time by not commuting. If I lived off campus, I'd have to fight traffic in the morning and then try to find a parking space somewhere. But living on campus would allow me simply to walk to class in the morning and to save a lot of time.

**Sample Response 2** Off Campus
02-50

The best option for me would be to live in off-campus housing, such as an apartment complex. I'd like to live off campus first because it would allow me to have more privacy. Dormitories usually require students to share a small room with a roommate and to use a public bathroom that dozens of other students also use. In an apartment, I'd have a private bedroom and bathroom. I'd also like off-campus living better because private apartments are more comfortable. Dorm rooms are notoriously small and Spartan, such as having brick walls painted white and very utilitarian furniture. Apartments, on the other hand, are designed to be cozier, which would be a more relaxing environment to go home to after a long day of classes.

### Task 2 | **Increased Parking Permit Fees**

### ◊ Reading
p.91

(**Prediction**) I think the speakers may be upset about the increase in parking permit fees.

**Critical Thinking:** Both changes discourage students from owning vehicles or driving on campus.

### ◊ Listening
p.92

Script 02-51

M: Can you believe this? Where do they get off charging 300 dollars for parking permits? College is already expensive enough, and now this?

W: It's upsetting, but I can understand it. There just aren't enough parking lots for everyone. This should help free up a lot of spaces.

M: I don't see how upping the price like this is going to create more parking spaces.

W: That's not what I mean. Obviously, the number of parking spaces will remain the same. But I think people who live nearby will take public transportation instead of driving.

M: I see where you're going with this. If fewer people drive to school, parking won't be so much of a problem.

W: Bingo. It'll be better for the planet, too. Too many people in the U.S. commute by car. If everyone would ride buses, we could really cut down on greenhouse gas emissions.

**M:** Maybe the price hike isn't such a bad thing overall even though I have no choice but to drive since I live an hour away.

**W:** Oh, come on. Three hundred dollars is a drop in the bucket compared to tuition and books. You'll manage.

---

(**Critical Analysis**)

1 My prediction was different than the actual response. I thought the speakers would be angry, but the woman felt the change was necessary and helpful.

2 The extra fees could be used to improve existing parking facilities.

3 I would not be happy about paying extra for parking, but since I plan to live on campus, I don't think it would affect me.

## Planning
p.93

**Woman's Opinion:** *The change is good.*

Reason 1: *more parking spaces*

Reason 2: *better for the environment*

## Grading
p.93

**Sample Response**
02-52

The two speakers are discussing the announced raise in parking permit fees, which are going up by twenty-five percent. The woman feels that the price hike is justified and will be helpful overall. She gives two reasons for her opinion. First, she says that it will help to free up more parking spaces. In her mind, some students who live near the university campus will take public transportation instead of paying for the more expensive parking permit. This will indirectly cause more of the parking spaces to be free for students who must drive. Second, she thinks that this change will help the environment. Since more people will be taking the bus instead of driving personal vehicles, there will be fewer greenhouse gas emissions generated by students. So the woman supports the increase because it will free up more parking spaces and benefit the environment.

---

## Task 3 | Business: The Productivity Paradox

## Reading
p.94

(**Prediction**) The lecture may be about various technologies that have slowed down productivity rather than increased it.

**Critical Thinking:** The main technology over the past decade has been the Internet. I believe it has dramatically increased productivity.

## Listening
p.95

**Script 02-53**

**Professor:** Last week, we talked about how the Internet has created new challenges for business managers. Today, we're going to take a different look at how the Internet has changed the workplace. It has come as a surprise that, overall, the Internet has increased employee productivity more than any other technology. But how can this be? Well, ah . . . that is a good question. People waste lots of time surfing the Net, right? Well, that's true, and it's not.

What research has shown is that updating social networking sites, checking email, reading news sites, and other non-work-related Internet activity give employees a little break. It gives their minds a moment or two to rest, and they are able to concentrate better when they get back to work. You know how fatigued you feel after a forty-five-minute lecture? But then you take a five- or ten-minute break between classes, and your brain is ready to go again, right? The Internet boosts productivity by the same principle.

The Internet also helps office workers accomplish tasks more efficiently. Think about how quickly you can find a phone number online compared to the time it takes to get a phonebook and find it that way. It's not even comparable, is it? So, umm . . . many different tasks are sped up because of the Internet.

---

(**Critical Analysis**)

1 The lecture is actually about technology that has increased productivity.

2 The lecture gives information that refutes the reading passage.

3 I think that photocopiers and fax machines have slowed down the time spent sending and copying documents, thus increasing productivity.

**Main Idea:** *The Internet increases productivity.*

Supporting Detail 1: *time to relax*

Supporting Detail 2: *accomplish tasks faster*

◈ **Grading**     p.96

**Sample Response**     02-54

The reading is about the productivity paradox, which states that office technology designed to increase productivity actually decreases it. The Internet is given as an example of a technology that defies the productivity paradox, and the professor elaborates on the reasons for this. First, he says that the Internet gives employees a chance to refresh their brains after long periods of work. He says that reading non-work-related websites such as news or social networking sites allows a person to relax for a few minutes. After the break, employees work with better efficiency. The professor compares this to students taking a short break between lectures. The professor also mentions that the Internet makes some tasks faster. You can easily find a phone number online much faster than you could if you had to find it in a phonebook.

Chapter **07** | Integrated Speaking

Task **4** | **The Arts: Dadaism**

◈ **Listening**     p.97

Script 02-55

Professor: Many people may look at Dadaist works and say, "That's not art." Well, they would be correct. Those involved in forming the Dada movement labeled their works anti-art. The movement was formed as a reaction to World War I, a war the Dadaists blamed on the cultural elite of the day. They attempted to fight back by causing chaos in the art world, which was dominated by the upper class. Everything the art world thought art should be, the Dadaists did exactly the opposite.

One of the first attempts to rattle the art world took place in 1917 in New York City. French artist Marcel Duchamp heard about a public exhibition that claimed to accept any works of art. He submitted a toilet, which he had signed with the name R. Mutt. As it turned out, the committee for the exhibition decided that the piece was not a work of art. It was later lost, presumably thrown out by mistake. Nevertheless, the piece was

reviewed by magazines, and the art world was shocked that someone would submit a toilet as a work of art.

Dada did not focus on visual arts alone but music and dance as well. In Paris, composer Erik Satie wrote a ballet entitled *Parade*. The ballet was performed by a famous Russian troupe, but it was no typical ballet. The dance moves were ridiculous and were obvious attempts to mock popular ballet. The music was changed, too. There were typical instruments—the piano, the violin, and so forth—but added to that mix were typewriters, foghorns, glass bottles, and other items that make noise but aren't normally considered musical instruments. These two elements combined caused quite a stir among the upper class, who took their music very seriously.

Critical Analysis

1 The professor uses two examples of Dadaist attacks against the upper class to show how the Dadaists attacked the cultural elite of their time.

2 The lecture implies that the art world was shaken by both examples given, so I'd say they were successful.

◈ **Planning**     p.98

**Main Idea:** *The Dadaists created anti-art to fight against the cultural elites of their time.*

Supporting Detail 1: *toilet submitted as art*

Supporting Detail 2: *ballet that had odd dance and music*

◈ **Grading**     p.98

**Sample Response**     02-56

The lecture is about the Dadaist movement. It was an art movement, but the professor states that it was created as anti-art, not as art. It began after World War I, when Dadaists wanted to attack the cultural elite, whom they blamed for the war. The professor explains how the Dadaists did this by giving two examples. The first example is from French Dadaist Marcel Duchamp. He heard about an art exhibition in New York City that would accept any submissions. He decided to submit something, but it was not art. It was a toilet. The piece was thrown away, but the art world was shaken because no one could believe someone would submit a toilet as art. The second example the professor gives is about ballet. Composer Erik Satie wrote a ballet that was performed by a Russian troupe. The ballet featured extremely odd dance moves and music that used regular instruments as well as non-instruments. This caused a stir in the music world since upper class music fans took ballet very seriously.

## Task 1 | Movie Theaters or Home Viewing

### ◈ Planning
p.100

**At Home**

Supporting Detail 1: *more comfortable*

Supporting Detail 2: *cheaper*

**At Theaters**

Supporting Detail 1: *part of a night out*

Supporting Detail 2: *example – recent story*

### ◈ Grading
p.100

**Sample Response 1** At Home                    02-57

To me, it is better to watch movies at home than to watch them in theaters. I feel this way for a couple of reasons. To start with, I'd say that my home is much more comfortable than any movie theater. In my living room, we have a big, comfortable sofa, which is nicer to sit on than a theater chair. And, of course, I don't have to worry about rude people talking loudly or using their cell phones in my living room. The other reason I like to watch movies at home is the cost. My family can stream movies on various services for just a few dollars. At a theater, we'd each need expensive tickets. So it's much cheaper to stream a movie and stay home.

**Sample Response 2** At Theaters                02-58

I very much prefer to watch movies at theaters rather than at home. I find it is a much more enjoyable experience and a part of a night out with friends. When you think of a night out, you think of going to dinner and a movie and maybe having coffee afterward. The movie is an important part of the night out. If you watch it at home, you will miss out on the experience of going out with your friends. To illustrate what I mean, a few weeks ago, a few friends and I met in the late afternoon. We had an enjoyable dinner together and then walked to the movie theater. We saw a comedy and laughed together with the audience. After the movie, we went to an ice cream shop and talked about the movie. Overall, it was a very enjoyable experience.

## Task 2 | Dining with the University President

### ◈ Reading
p.101

(**Prediction**) I think the speakers will talk about what they want to say to the president.

**Critical Thinking:** I would like to talk about what problems I am experiencing at the school and ask for helping in fixing them.

### ◈ Listening
p.102

Script 02-59

W: I just checked my e-mail. I'll be having lunch with the president next week.

M: You must be really excited about that.

W: On the contrary, I couldn't care less. I'm graduating this spring, so it's kind of pointless to meet the president now.

M: I feel the opposite. I'm having dinner with him next month, and I'm looking forward to it.

W: Why is that?

M: Well, first of all, he's one of the greatest inventors of our time. Before he became the president, he ran his own laboratory. I'd love to hear him talk about some of his inventions.

W: That's interesting. I never knew that about him.

M: Plus, I'd love to make a couple of suggestions about how we can improve the school. You know, uh, it's hard to schedule a meeting with the president because he's so busy. But I'll be able to talk to him at dinner and let him know what I'd do to make the school better.

(**Critical Analysis**)

1   I was correct about what the man would say, but the woman is not interested in speaking with the president.

2   At first, she has no interest in talking to the school president, but later, she thinks it might be interesting to speak with him.

3   He might want to discuss classes, professors, or school life with the president.

### ◈ Planning
p.103

**Man's Opinion:** *He is pleased to dine with the president.*

Reason 1: *president was a great inventor*

*Reason 2: wants to discuss school improvements*

## ◈ Grading

p.103

**Sample Response**                                    02-60

- - - - - - - - - - - - - - - - - - - - - - - - - - - - - - - - - - - - -

The students are having a conversation about an announcement by the school. According to the announcement, all students at the school will be able to have either lunch or dinner with the university president. They will therefore be able to talk to him about various topics while they eat. The man is pleased with the announcement and is looking forward to having dinner with the president. The first reason he gives is that the president is a great inventor. He made many inventions in the past, and the man wants to hear the president talk about those inventions. The second reason he provides is that he has some ideas on how he would make the school better. Because he will be dining with the president, he will have the opportunity to bring up these ideas during dinner. Then, he will be able to suggest to the president how to improve the school.

---

**Chapter 08 | Integrated Speaking**

## Task 3 | Health: Pandemics

## ◈ Reading

p.104

(**Prediction**) The professor will give examples of pandemics to explain the concept.

**Critical Thinking:** Novel diseases can be introduced by foreigners, native residents returning from travel abroad, or animals.

## ◈ Listening

p.105

Script 02-61

**Professor:** Throughout human history, diseases have worked to keep the world population in check. Now, each year, people all over the place die from various diseases. But a disease doesn't really have a devastating impact until it becomes a pandemic. For example, the 1918 flu pandemic, more commonly known as, ah . . . the Spanish Flu, spread to every continent and infected a third of the world's population.

No one is sure exactly where this strain of the flu originated, but most scholars agree it spread so quickly due to World War I. As infected soldiers continued to mingle with one another and with civilians in foreign lands rather than stay at home as people normally do when they are sick, the strain was able to travel across the globe while infecting one population at a time.

The effect of this flu was drastic. As I said before, a third of the world's population was infected. This led to some seventeen million people dying in India, which was, um, about five percent of its population at that time. But this is nothing compared to the tragedy some parts of Alaska and Southern Africa experienced, where the disease killed off entire villages.

(Critical Analysis)

1   The lecture was about one example of a pandemic, so my prediction was mostly accurate.

2   The reading defines a concept while the listening explains the concept in further detail by using a specific example.

3   H1N1, or Swine Flu, became a pandemic in 2009.

## ◈ Planning

p.106

**Main Idea:** *pandemic = new disease; devastating impact*

Supporting Detail 1: *Spanish Flu, spread by soldiers*

Supporting Detail 2: *dead – 17 million in India, villages in Alaska & Southern Africa*

## ◈ Grading

p.106

**Sample Response**                                    02-62

- - - - - - - - - - - - - - - - - - - - - - - - - - - - - - - - - - - - -

According to the reading passage, a pandemic occurs when a novel disease spreads throughout large areas of land and has a devastating impact on societies. The professor explains this concept by talking about the Spanish Flu of 1918, which is an example of a pandemic. This flu was spread around the world by soldiers who were fighting in World War I. Unlike people who normally stay at home when they are ill, the soldiers continued to travel around the world even though they had the flu. This caused the disease to be spread to people in many different countries. The result that it had was devastating for several countries. The professor mentions a few in particular. India experienced a five-percent loss of its population with about seventeen million people dying from the flu. She also says that some entire villages in Alaska and Africa were killed by the disease.

## Task 4 | Education: Literacy in Education

### ◈ Listening
p.107

Script 02-63

**Professor:** The methods of education used during Hellenic Greece were quite different from the educational models of today. Students were expected to memorize epic poems and other works and to be able to recall them immediately. Information was chiefly transmitted orally, but around the time of Plato, there began a movement to use writing. It's interesting that some folks at the time opposed the use of writing in education. Plato actually argued two main points against it.

First, Plato said that written information was, ah, what he called "the third place from the truth." He meant that truth, or the first step, was the original thought, and the writer putting his thoughts into words was one step away. Then, when we read those words, we are three steps away. This was important to Plato primarily because the reader can never fully understand the writer's thoughts and thus gains little truth from the experience. He explains further by saying that the reader cannot question the thinker and is thus unable to apply the Socratic method of cross-examination in order to discover the truth.

His second attack on literacy has to do with what I mentioned earlier about how students of the day memorized poems and tales of incredible lengths. In ancient Greece, it was crucial that someone memorize a vast number of works to be able to debate coherently in the public forum. Plato argued that if people began to rely on reading and writing rather than on memory and oral recall, then our ability to memorize things would be greatly diminished. When we consider that educated people of the day could memorize Homer's *Odyssey*, which is some 12,000 lines long, we begin to see that Plato may have been on to something.

#### Critical Analysis

1 Literacy allows a greater variety of information to be transmitted easily and to be preserved accurately forever.

2 He was correct that we cannot question the writer, and I think this is something modern journalists especially need to keep in mind when they write.

### ◈ Planning
p.108

**Main idea:** *Hellenic Greece – oral culture; Plato opposed writing*

Supporting Detail 1: *is the third place from truth*

Supporting Detail 2: *diminishes the memory*

### ◈ Grading
p.108

**Sample Response** 02-64

The professor begins the lecture by stating that education during Hellenic Greece was mostly oral. Students memorized long poems and other information so that they could easily recall it. Around this time, writing began to be introduced, but some people opposed it. The professor uses the arguments of Plato to represent those who opposed literacy. He said that Plato had two main arguments. His first argument was that literacy was "three places from the truth." The truth is the mind of the writer. Once he writes, the writing becomes the second place. Others reading those words are the third place. Since cross-examination was important in the oral culture of ancient Greece, Plato saw writing as less truthful and therefore less beneficial than speaking. Plato's second argument was that people's memory capacities would be reduced due to literacy. Since people of his day memorized epic poems such as the *Odyssey*, the professor thinks Plato had a good point.

## Task 1 | Vacation Destinations

### ◈ Planning
p.110

**New Destination**

Supporting Detail 1: *a sense of adventure*

Supporting Detail 2: *cultural exposure*

**Same Destination**

Supporting Detail 1: *less stressful – know the place and can just relax*

Supporting Detail 2: *example – a beach town in Japan*

### ◈ Grading
p.110

**Sample Response 1** New Destination 02-65

When I travel, I prefer to go to a new location every trip. There are two main reasons I prefer this. To start, I have a strong sense of adventure. I love eating different kinds of food, meeting different people, doing new things, and especially visiting new places. When I go to a place I've never visited, the feeling of excitement I get cannot be compared to anything else. This brings me to my other reason, which is that I love to learn about different cultures as much as possible. I think traveling to new places is the best way to do that. Last year, my family visited Vietnam. While the Vietnamese share some customs with my home country, I was very interested in observing the differences between us.

**Sample Response 2** Same Destination                  02-66

In my opinion, it's better to find a place you enjoy and stick with it. The main reason I think this is that the purpose of a vacation is to relax and to escape the stress and the worries of your regular life. If you travel to new places, there is a lot of stress in finding hotels, understanding the public transportation system, and finding restaurants. But if you know the place well, you can simply relax and enjoy your vacation without any extra stress. To illustrate this point, my family often travels to a small beach town in Japan. We have been there many times, so we know the neighbors and the local shopkeepers, we know exactly where to go if we want a night out, and we've even learned some of the local language.

Chapter **09** | Integrated Speaking

Task 2 | **Department Budget Cuts**

◊ **Reading**                                     p.111

(**Prediction**) I think the speakers may be involved with the Department of Economics and will be upset about the budget cut.

**Critical Thinking:** The university will no longer offer an important area of study, which could discourage student attendance.

◊ **Listening**                                   p.112

Script 02-67

M: My international business professor was talking about this budget cut today. She said she's glad her department wasn't cut.

W: That's great for her, but think about what a cut like this is going to do to the College of Business in

general.

M: What do you mean?

W: A lot of business majors take economics classes as part of their required coursework. For example, I am working on a minor in accounting. As part of that, I have to take some basic economics courses.

M: That's true. I hadn't really thought about that. So are students in related business majors going to have major scheduling conflicts because of this change?

W: Yes, I imagine they'll cut those courses and redesign some of the programs. And think about how this is going to affect our school's reputation. Our business program is going to be seen as inferior to others if it doesn't include economics.

M: And what good is a degree if employers consider it worthless?

(**Critical Analysis**)

1    The woman is affected because she is a business major, so my prediction is similar to what the dialogue said.

2    She may not have valuable economics knowledge that she could need in business or at graduate school.

3    The budget will suffer in the long run if enrollment drops due to the loss of the department.

◊ **Planning**                                    p.113

**Woman's Opinion:** *She is upset about the cut.*

Reason 1: *will disrupt current programs*

Reason 2: *will hurt the university's business program image*

◊ **Grading**                                     p.113

**Sample Response**                               02-68

The two students are talking about the planned cutting of the Department of Economics from the university's College of Business. The female student agrees with the letter written by Professor Ross and is upset about the announcement. First, she mentions that she is a business major and that she has to take economics courses in order to finish her program. With the loss of the department, she will probably need to redesign her program and will perhaps have scheduling conflicts as a result. Second, she worries that the university's image as a whole will be tarnished due to the change. She states that her university will be seen as inferior for business, which will diminish the perceived value of a degree from the school. In other words, the woman thinks that cutting the Department of Economics will make studying difficult for current students and devalue her college degree.

## Task 3 | Economics: Monopoly Markets

### ◊ Reading
p.114

**(Prediction)** The lecturer will talk about some problems with monopoly markets and maybe give an example of one.

**Critical Thinking:** Monopoly markets might result in very high prices for goods that are needed by people, so people will have to spend a lot of money to acquire them.

### ◊ Listening
p.115

Script 02-69

**Professor:** We all know that monopolies are undesirable. At least, that's what we're taught at school. But have you ever thought about why people dislike monopoly markets?

Here's a personal example. Last month, I had to fly to another city to attend a conference. I decided to depart from our local airport, which isn't particularly big. It only has ten gates. Well, I got there early and was hungry, so I decided to buy something to eat. However, there was a huge problem.

You see, there's just one restaurant in the airport. It sells sandwiches. I got there and checked out the menu. You wouldn't believe the prices being charged for sandwiches. The cheapest one was twelve dollars, and a couple were listed at twenty dollars. That was simply way too much. In addition, there was a long, long line. At least thirty people were waiting to order. It took the staff at the restaurant approximately four or five minutes to get each customer some food. I couldn't wait that long because my flight was leaving in an hour. Unfortunately, there were no other options since that's the only place in the airport to purchase food. Do you know what I did? I went hungry. It just wasn't worth the wait or the price. And that's why monopoly markets are undesirable.

1   The professor gave a personal example and explained some problems with monopoly markets, so my prediction was accurate.

2   He does this to give the students a personal example to help them understand some problems with monopoly markets.

3   The professor would have to wait a very long time in line at the restaurant and pay a high price for his food. Because there were no other restaurants, he had no choice on where to eat, which is a big problem.

### ◊ Planning
p.116

**Main Idea:** *monopoly markets – only one seller but many buyers; many disadvantages*

**Supporting Detail 1:** *very high prices at the only restaurant*

**Supporting Detail 2:** *long wait in line; didn't have time before flight departed*

### ◊ Grading
p.116

**Sample Response**
02-70

The professor tells the students about what happened a month ago when he decided to fly out of the local airport. He says he got to the airport early and was hungry, so he decided to get something to eat. However, there is only one restaurant in the entire airport. First, he noticed the prices of the sandwiches were very expensive. Second, he saw that there were around thirty people waiting in line, and the serving times were several minutes for each person. He was both unwilling and unable to pay the high prices and to wait in line for that long, so he went hungry. The situation at the airport is an example of a monopoly market. This happens when there is one seller of a product but many buyers. The monopolist is able to charge any desired price for the product, and buyers must pay for it or go without it.

## Task 4 | Geology: Dating Fossils

### ◊ Listening
p.117

Script 02-71

**Professor:** I'm sure many of you have heard in the news that a much smaller cousin of the T. Rex was found in

China recently. They've dated it at having lived roughly ninety million years ago, which is about thirty-five million years earlier than the T. Rex. I bring this up because I want to, uh, explain how it is that paleontologists come up with these dates. There are two main processes that they use.

The oldest method of dating fossils was a process that we call stratigraphy. See, uh, the Earth's crust is made up of layers of rock, called strata, that are created by sediment or lava—things like that—over millions of years. These strata are distinct from one another. The lower the stratum, the older the rock, as well as anything found in the rocks. Based on which stratum a fossil is found in, scientists are able to determine its relative age. So fossils found in upper strata are known to be younger than fossils found in lower strata. But stratigraphy does not tell us exactly how old a fossil is. That's where radiometric dating comes into play. The rocks in strata contain certain isotopes that are radioactive. Scientists are able to take a sample of isotopes found in the rocks around a fossil and find out how much of it has decayed. Based on this information, they can determine the approximate age of a fossil.

( Critical Analysis )

1  I think that layers of sediment and lava are built up over time when new rocks or lava fall down and cover the existing ones.

2  Stratigraphy is similar to counting the rings of a tree. As you go further to the center of the tree trunk, you add years of age to the tree. This is like counting down through strata.

## ◊ Planning
p.118

**Main Idea:** *Dating fossils – two main methods*

Supporting Detail 1: *stratigraphy – counting the strata of the Earth's crust*

Supporting Detail 2: *radiometric dating – isotope decay*

## ◊ Grading
p.118

### Sample Response
02-72

The lecture opens with a reference to a cousin of the T. Rex that was found. The professor mentions this discovery because she wants to introduce the topic of dating fossils. She says that there are two primary methods that paleontologists use to date fossils. The first method she discusses is called stratigraphy. This involves counting through the layers of the Earth's crust.

There are layers called strata, which are made up of sediment and lava. When fossils are found, scientists look at the stratum they were found in. The deeper the stratum, the older the fossils are. But the professor says this only gives us the relative ages of fossils. To get a better approximation, scientists use radiometric dating. This is done by looking at isotopes in rocks around fossils. Based on how much the isotopes have decayed, scientists can determine the approximate ages of fossils in a stratum.

## Task 1 | **Foreign Language Requirement**

## ◊ Planning
p.120

### Agree

Supporting Detail 1: *learn about other cultures – global society*

Supporting Detail 2: *develops part of the brain like math does*

### Disagree

Supporting Detail 1: *is not needed for most jobs*

Supporting Detail 2: *requires too much effort*

## ◊ Grading
p.120

### Sample Response 1  Agree
02-73

I agree that high school students ought to take foreign language courses in order to graduate. The first reason is that studying a foreign language teaches one about more than just a language. You also learn about foreign cultures. It's impossible to learn a language without learning about the cultures that use that language. Since we live in a global society today, it is more important than ever to appreciate and value people with different traditions, so learning about foreign languages and cultures is vital to all high school students. The second reason is that the purpose of high school is to help cultivate a young person's mind in every way possible. Studying a foreign language helps people develop a part of their brain in the same way that math, science, and history do.

### Sample Response 2  Disagree
02-74

Personally, I'm against the foreign language requirement for high school students to graduate. Foreign languages are nice, and being fluent in two or three languages could be a good skill to have, but for most people, it is not useful in their everyday lives. High school is a way to prepare for college, which prepares us for good jobs, but the great majority of jobs do not require any foreign language proficiency. Unlike knowledge of math or society, foreign languages really won't benefit most people in their careers. In addition to this, I think foreign languages require much more dedication to learn than other subjects do. Countless hours must be spent memorizing vocabulary and practicing grammar, which leaves students with less time to study other subjects like math and history.

---

Chapter **10** | Integrated Speaking

## Task 2 | New Cafeteria Meal Plans

### ◈ Reading
p.121

(Prediction) I think one of the speakers will be someone who eats at the cafeteria three times a day and is upset about the increase in the price.

**Critical Thinking:** Students could save money if they only eat at the cafeteria once or twice a day.

### ◈ Listening
p.122

Script 02-75

W: Oh, check this out. I was wondering when our school's cafeteria was going to change its archaic meal plan options.

M: You don't think this is a good thing, do you?

W: Of course I do. Most students I know don't eat breakfast there, and a lot of times I skip lunch because I'm too busy with my classes to take a break. Why pay for something I don't use?

M: But look at the higher prices. An extra dollar per meal is an exorbitant price hike. They could have just changed the meal plans, but instead they've decided to gouge us on the prices while they're at it.

W: I don't look at it that way. Sure, the individual meals may be pricier, but the overall savings from only paying for the meals you eat will more than cover the higher cost. Just think: Instead of spending twelve dollars a day when I may only eat one meal there, I can pay four fifty a day and have the same meal. That's a savings of seven fifty.

---

(Critical Analysis)

1　The woman's opinion is opposite of what I predicted, but the man seems to be upset about the price hike, possibly because he eats three meals a day at the cafeteria.

2　Many students probably skip breakfast because they don't wake up early enough.

3　I think the price of meals was raised because the cafeteria needs to make up for the loss of revenue when students mix and match meal plans.

### ◈ Planning
p.123

**Woman's Opinion:** *She is happy about the change.*

Reason 1: *many students skip meals*

Reason 2: *save money*

### ◈ Grading
p.123

**Sample Response**
02-76

The two students are discussing changes to the university's cafeteria meal plans. The new plan will allow students to mix and match how many meals they want to purchase, but this will come with a price hike of one dollar per meal. The female student is happy about the change to the old plan, which she feels is outdated and in need of improvement. She first says that under the current plan, she and other students are paying for meals they don't eat. For example, most students she knows don't eat breakfast, and she often skips lunch because she is too busy. With the new plan, she can choose to pay for only the meals she eats. She goes on to say that she thinks the new plan will give her an overall savings in cost. The price per meal will go up, but since she will purchase fewer meals, the total cost will end up being less than what it was under the old plan.

---

Chapter **10** | Integrated Speaking

## Task 3 | Urban Studies: Urban Sprawl

### ◈ Reading
p.124

(Prediction) I predict that the lecturer will focus on how personal vehicles and urban sprawl can negatively affect the environment.

**Critical Thinking:** There might be an increase in pollution due to everyone driving personal vehicles instead of using public transportation.

**Professor:** Today, we're going to talk about the growing prevalence of suburban lifestyles, known as urban sprawl, specifically how they, ah . . . the negative effects they produce.

First and foremost is the problem of obesity. Take a trip through any suburb, and you'll see that most people are overweight, especially compared to people in the city. That's due to the distances caused by urban sprawl. Let's say you need to run some errands. By car, it's a fifteen-minute drive to the supermarket. The bank is a ten-minute drive from there. You want to visit the library, and that's another ten-minute drive. Then, you drive twenty minutes to get home. This would be an all-day task if you had to walk or even ride a bike. So everyone drives. There really aren't any places you can walk or ride a bike to in the suburbs. It's easy to see that, um, that a lifestyle that includes very little aerobic exercise will lead to higher levels of obesity.

The second problem I'd like to mention is that of the water supply. What was once undeveloped natural land is now ground covered with impervious surfaces, such as asphalt and concrete. Less water is able to reach aquifers deep underground. This, along with an increased demand for water, results in lower water tables in suburban areas.

**Critical Analysis**

1 The lecture is similar to my prediction, but only one of the negative effects mentioned is related to the environment.

2 I think the distances are useful in isolating the pollution of industrial areas and the crime associated with commercial areas.

3 The high dependence on personal vehicles will cause runoff water to be more highly polluted.

◈ **Planning** p.126

**Main Idea:** *urban sprawl – negative effects*

Supporting Detail 1: *obesity – personal vehicles; no exercise*

Supporting Detail 2: *lower water tables*

Urban sprawl is the growing trend of people moving out of cities and into residential areas called suburbs. The suburbs are defined by isolated areas of commerce, residence, and industry, and most people there drive personal vehicles instead of taking public transportation. The professor explains the concept further by introducing two problems that can result from urban sprawl. The first problem he mentions is obesity. He explains that a large proportion of people in the suburbs are obese because of their dependence on driving. Since locations are so far apart, there is no way that people can ride bicycles or walk to where they need to go. This lack of exercise results in higher rates of obesity. The second problem the professor mentions concerns diminishing water tables in suburban areas. The land is mostly covered in asphalt, which is impervious to water, so less water is able to make it down to the aquifers. That problem is compounded by a higher demand for water in suburban areas.

Chapter **10** | Integrated Speaking

## Task 4 | **Agriculture: Crossbreeding**

◈ **Listening** p.127

Script 02-79

**Professor:** Nearly all of the major crop plants we use today are the results of thousands of years of selective breeding. That is, farmers use seeds from only the best plants to weed out the bad ones. But our crops have been improved even more with crossbreeding. This is the practice of using two varieties of plants within the same species to create a new variety. Crossbreeding has allowed farmers to create crops that are better in quality and more useful to humans. Let's take a look at the strawberry. People around the world love this juicy red fruit, but it wasn't always so desirable. Wild strawberries are much smaller—about the size of a dime—and they aren't always, uh, quite so sweet. When settlers came to America in the 1500s, they saw that the Native Americans had been selectively breeding strawberries that were much better than European varieties. They learned from the Native Americans how to grow these strawberries and eventually began to crossbreed them with European varieties. The strawberries you know today are the direct results of hundreds of years of crossbreeding.

Crossbreeding has also been used to stop famines and to prevent starvation. In the 1960s, India was experiencing one of its worst-ever famines. But by the end of the decade, the problem had been solved. How was this possible? Well, it had to do with the use of newly developed rice seeds. See, these rice seeds had been crossbred to produce a higher crop yield. The new rice plants were able to produce double the yield of the old plants. This solved the hunger crisis not only in India but also in Pakistan and other countries.

( Critical Analysis )

1 Based on implications in the lecture, I expect that wild strawberries that have not been crossbred will be smaller and less juicy than the ones we buy at grocery stores.

2 Higher crop yield means that more crops can be harvested from the same number of plants. When arable farmland is limited, higher crop yields produce more food overall, ending starvation.

## ◈ Planning
p.128

**Main Idea:** *crossbreeding – is useful to humans*

Supporting Detail 1: *better food produced by weeding out bad*

Supporting Detail 2: *used to end famine – India*

## ◈ Grading
p.128

**Sample Response**
02-80

The topic of the lecture is the crossbreeding of plants, which involves using two varieties of a species to make a new one. This allows farmers to make plants that are of better quality and to weed out plants that are not as useful. The professor explains crossbreeding by explaining two ways that it benefits humans. The first point he makes is that crossbreeding allows us to have better quality food. To illustrate this point, he gives the example of strawberries. Original European strawberries were smaller and not very sweet. They were later crossbred with American strawberries that had been selectively bred by Native Americans. After a few hundred years, modern strawberries were developed. The professor also discusses the point of using crossbreeding to stop famine. This point is also explained with the help of an example. In India in the 1960s, there was a terrible famine. A new type of rice seed that produced a greater crop yield was developed, and this ended the famine.

## Task 1 | **Purpose of University Study**

### ◈ Planning
p.130

**Agree**

Supporting Detail 1: *high cost – need a payoff to justify the expense*

Supporting Detail 2: *university is only useful for career training*

**Disagree**

Supporting Detail 1: *helps develop one's mind – is useful in everyday life*

Supporting Detail 2: *can prepare one generally for one's future plans*

### ◈ Grading
p.130

**Sample Response 1** Agree
02-81

I'd definitely agree that one should attend university as a way to prepare for one's career. To begin with, university costs can be quite expensive when you add up tuition, books, and living expenses. The expense is so great that students often go into debt with student loans. The only way to justify such massive expenses is to use your time at university as a way to prepare yourself for a career that requires a degree. Furthermore, if one does not intend to begin a career that requires a degree, there is no reason to attend university. If a degree is not needed, it would be better to save your time and to begin preparing for whatever path you wish to take.

**Sample Response 2** Disagree
02-82

In my opinion, one does not need a specific career in mind when deciding to attend university. The first reason for my opinion is that I believe university can develop a person's mind. University-level courses are challenging, and the required effort helps a person develop critical thinking and analytical skills. These are skills that can be useful to someone even if that person never starts a career. I'd also point to the fact that many students don't know what they want to do. By exposing themselves to various topics and earning a general degree, students can narrow down their career options and eventually choose something they'd like to pursue. That's why I think it isn't necessary to attend university only to prepare for a specific career.

## Task 2 | Classes Relocated

### ◊ Reading
p.131

(**Prediction**) I think the students will be excited about the changes due to the improvements in the engineering building.

**Critical Thinking:** The immediate downsides are that students will be relocated to another building that does not have the technology and equipment they may need and that students may be inconvenienced by having to go to another building.

### ◊ Listening
p.132

Script 02-83

M: Oh, it looks like we've got to go to the math and science building.

W: Gosh, what a burden. We just walked all the way over here, and now we have to walk somewhere else.

M: That's a little annoying, but just think: Most of our classes are in that building, so this will save us time in the long run. On Monday, Wednesday, and Friday, all my classes will be in that one building. What a convenience!

W: I guess what I'm really peeved about is that we're going to lose access to the computers and equipment we need. We're only sophomores, so we're learning the basics of engineering. I just hope this doesn't affect our ability to gain a solid foundational knowledge of engineering.

M: I'm sure Dr. Norris has thought of that. Besides, we'll have a stellar building when the work is finished. By the time we're in advanced courses, we'll have access to the best facilities around, which will put us ahead of the competition.

(**Critical Analysis**)

1   My prediction was similar since one of the students is excited about the change. The female student is not very happy about it.

2   No, he doesn't. Her main complaint is about the lack of equipment, but he responds that their professor most likely made plans to deal with that.

3   Students will be able to learn with cutting-edge technology that they may need to use when they get jobs after graduation.

### ◊ Planning
p.133

**Man's Opinion:** *He is happy about the change.*

Reason 1: *is easier for him – has classes in the same building*

Reason 2: *will be better for future studies*

### ◊ Grading
p.133

**Sample Response**                                   02-84

The man and the woman have just read an announcement from their engineering professor about their class's relocation while the engineering building is under reconstruction. The man is practically elated by the announcement for two reasons. First, his classes on Monday, Wednesday, and Friday are all in the math and science building, where his engineering class is being relocated to. He says this will save him time and be an added convenience for him. So he is happy about the temporary classroom relocation. He continues by saying why he is happy to wait for the renovations to be completed. According to the man, although the students will miss out on computers and technology for now, by the time they are in advanced courses, they will have the best equipment for studying. He feels this will give the students an edge against engineering students at other universities.

## Task 3 | Earth Science: Biodiversity

### ◊ Reading
p.134

(**Prediction**) I think the professor may explain biodiversity by giving examples of various organisms and their habitats.

**Critical Thinking:** The various types of plants that exist on land and in the water help supply us with oxygen and break down greenhouse gases in the atmosphere.

### ◊ Listening
p.135

Script 02-85

**Professor:** In our last class, we talked about biodiversity and why it is important to us as humans. Today, we'll look at what we humans are doing to, well, shoot ourselves in the foot, so to speak. Though we benefit from biodiversity, our very behavior is killing off species at an alarming rate.

Perhaps the greatest threat to mammal populations posed by humans throughout history has been overhunting. Some animals are hunted because they are highly prized and their parts can fetch high prices. In Africa, rhinoceroses are hunted for their horns, which can sell for upward of 100,000 dollars apiece. But other animals are overhunted primarily for the meat and the skin they provide. This is precisely the reason why buffalo here in America nearly went extinct in the nineteenth century. Native Americans and settlers alike overhunted them until there were only a few hundred left. Then there's the issue of habitat loss. This is the hidden species killer, and one we don't often consider, but it's, ah, perhaps the most . . . destructive human behavior. This happens when we clear out great areas of forest to build settlements or to create farmland. The endemic organisms that existed on the land prior to its conversion either flee or die. Eventually, there is nowhere left for mobile organisms to run to, and their population numbers dwindle as a result.

### Critical Analysis

1   The lecture was different because it focused on how humans are hurting biodiversity rather than elaborating on what biodiversity is.

2   Because biodiversity benefits us as humans, we are only hurting ourselves when we do things to weaken it.

3   Overhunting targets specific mammals, but habitat loss affects every organism existing in an affected area.

## ◈ Planning
p.136

**Main Idea:** *Biodiversity is hurt by human activity.*

Supporting Detail 1: *overhunting*

Supporting Detail 2: *habitat loss*

## ◈ Grading
p.136

### Sample Response
02-86

Biodiversity is the total collection of all species existing on the Earth. It is something that is important to humans because we benefit by having a multitude of sources of food, medicine, inspiration for art, and pillars of climate stability. The professor focuses his lecture on how humans are hurting themselves by damaging biodiversity through destructive behavior. The professor explains his argument by giving two examples of destructive behavior. He first talks about the problem of overhunting, which is when an animal is hunted to

extinction. People do this either because they can sell parts of an animal for a large sum or because they eat the animal for food. As a result, the rhinoceros and the American buffalo have been the victims of overhunting. The professor also uses the example of habitat loss. This occurs when humans clear out natural land to make buildings or farms. As a result of this action, organisms on the land must flee if they can or risk dying. In both of these ways, humans cause organism populations to dwindle.

Chapter **11** | Integrated Speaking

## Task 4 | Chemistry: Electron Configuration

## ◈ Listening
p.137

Script 02-87

**Professor:** In my last lecture, I explained to you the basic properties of an atom, including its neutrons, protons, and electrons. Today, I'd like to go a little more in depth on this topic by talking about electron configuration and why it's so important in chemistry.

So the first thing to note is that electrons orbit the atom's nucleus in what we call shells. The more electrons an atom has, the more shells it has. The shell farthest from the nucleus is called the valence shell. All the other shells are called inner shells. Now, ah . . . each shell can only hold a certain number of electrons. We'll get into the details of that later, but for now, um, just note that the farther an electron is from the atom, the weaker its energy level is.

Now, you might ask why this is important to chemistry. Okay, I told you that the weaker electrons are the ones farthest from the nucleus, which would be what shell? Yes, the valence shell. These electrons are the ones that are responsible for chemical bonding since their energy level is relatively weak. Most atoms do not have a full valence shell. What this means is that they will easily bond with other atoms in order to create a stable valence shell. Atoms that are missing one or two electrons or that have one or two extra electrons are especially reactive, forming bonds quite easily. Atoms with full valence shells, on the other hand, are quite stable and thus do not tend to form compounds naturally. Without this knowledge of electron configuration, then atomic compounds—a key element of chemistry—would be beyond our understanding.

1   The purpose of this lecture is to give students an overview of electron configuration while details will be provided later.

2   An atom that is unstable because of too few or too many electrons would be best for forming compounds since its valence shell is not full.

## ◈ Planning                                    p.138

**Main Idea:** *electron configuration – is responsible for compounds*

Supporting Detail 1: *layers of electrons; valence shell weakest*

Supporting Detail 2: *valence shell determines the ease of bonding*

## ◈ Grading                                     p.138

### Sample Response                              02-88

The purpose of the lecture is to explain how electrons are configured in an atom and why that is important to chemistry. The professor's first point is about electron configuration. She explains that electrons are arranged in shells and that the number of shells depends on how many electrons there are. The outer shell is called the valence shell. Not only is it the weakest electron shell in an atom, but it is also usually not full so is therefore unstable. Atoms seek to become stable by forming compounds with other atoms because the valence shell looks for extra electrons in order to become stable. This information about how compounds are formed, the professor says, is a key element of chemistry and something we could not understand without knowing about electron configuration.

Chapter **12** | Independent Speaking

## Task 1 | Public Funding of Museums

## ◈ Planning                                    p.140

**Public**

Supporting Detail 1: *private funding is not enough*
Supporting Detail 2: *benefit society*

**Private Funding**

Supporting Detail 1: *not everyone goes to museums*
Supporting Detail 2: *an unnecessary use of tax money*

## ◈ Grading                                     p.140

### Sample Response 1   Public                   02-89

I agree with the opinion that art museums should be publicly funded. I have a couple of reasons for my opinion. The first reason is that private funding is often not enough to keep museums open. The expenses involved in buying art, hiring curators and other employees, and maintaining the building can be quite costly. If all museums had to rely on private funding, many would end up closing down. My second reason is that I think art is something that benefits society as a whole. Publicly funded museums give citizens places to go where they can appreciate the beauty of life and find inspiration. Not only that, but museums improve a city's reputation and bring in tourists who help the local economy.

### Sample Response 2   Private Funding          02-90

I cannot agree with the opinion that art museums should be publicly funded. The main reason I feel this way is that not everyone goes to museums. Personally, I have only been to museums during school trips, and I would never visit one on my own. Many other people are disinterested in art and don't go to museums. So I believe that government money shouldn't be used to provide entertainment that only some people enjoy. In addition, I think that museums are a waste of tax money. In my view, taxes should be used for things that are necessary for a society to function, such as schools, roads, and defense. Spending millions of dollars on art museums does not improve society or make it more stable, so it is a waste of tax money.

Chapter **12** | Integrated Speaking

## Task 2 | Controversial Speaker

## ◈ Reading                                     p.141

**Prediction**   I think the speakers will discuss the positive and negative points of allowing Mr. Harper to speak at the university.

**Critical Thinking:** The controversial figure may encourage students to research an issue they may not have otherwise given much thought to.

M: I have to agree with this writer. The university shouldn't allow people like this to come speak to students.

W: Why not? The university is a place to exchange ideas. Even if you don't agree with what someone has to say, it's an opportunity for people to have a public debate and to decide on issues for themselves.

M: It's just a bad idea all around. I'm all for free speech and the free flow of ideas, but this is going too far. Someone like Harper should be shunned, not supported.

W: But that would be thought control. Look… I think it would be a good thing for the university. Sure, Harper doesn't have the best public image, but I think he'll help make the environment a hot issue on campus. In the end, I think we will see more activism on campus as a result of the debate he starts here.

( **Critical Analysis** )

1   The speakers responded roughly in the same way that I predicted.

2   He thinks Mr. Harper's views are too extreme, and he agrees with the writer that Mr. Harper is a domestic terrorist.

3   She means that not allowing Mr. Harper to speak would be the same as the university telling students what they can think and believe.

◈ **Planning**    p.143

**Woman's Opinion:** *She disagrees with the letter.*

Reason 1: *fosters public debate*

Reason 2: *will promote environmental activism*

◈ **Grading**    p.143

**Sample Response**    02-92

- - - - - - - - - - - - - - - - - - - - - - - - - - - - - - -

The woman and the man are talking about a letter to the editor in which the writer stated that a controversial figure should not be allowed to speak at the university. The letter claimed that the speaker is a radical environmentalist who is involved with domestic terrorism. The female student in the listening disagrees with the letter, saying that the controversial figure should be allowed to speak on campus. She gives two reasons

for her opinion. Her first reason is that she thinks a university is a place where ideas should be exchanged freely and without restriction. She thinks it would be good to have an open debate about the speaker's opinions. Her second reason is that she believes the speaker will promote the cause of environmentalism on the campus. She feels that more students will become involved in activism as a result of the speaker's appearance.

Task 3 | **American History: The Temperance Movement**

◈ **Reading**    p.144

( **Prediction** )  The reading passage defines the early Temperance Movement, so I predict the lecture will focus on what the movement grew to become.

**Critical Thinking:** I think they may have held protests and written letters to their representatives.

◈ **Listening**    p.145

Script 02-93

**Professor:** We all know about the Prohibition Era of U.S. history, but something you may not know is that women were a driving force behind its roots. Women saw alcoholism as destroying their marriages and families and thus took active roles, from the radical to the mainstream, in ridding it from society.

Perhaps the biggest figure in the temperance movement was Carrie Nation. She got involved in the movement in a major way when, in 1900, she began traveling to taverns and carrying out physical assaults on them. Nation began by throwing rocks at decorations in taverns to destroy their interiors, but she later took a more aggressive approach with an axe. That's right; she actually destroyed furniture and liquor kegs with an axe! She was arrested over thirty times for her actions, but she never gave up.

But Nation was not a leader; she was on the fringe of the movement. In the mainstream were women, mostly organized by the Women's Christian Temperance Union, who went to their local taverns and demonstrated outside by chanting slogans and singing hymns. They also encouraged their children not to drink and taught their daughters that a man who drank alcohol even moderately was the worst possible candidate for marriage.

1 My prediction was a little off. The lecture focuses on women's involvement in the movement and not just on how the movement evolved.

2 Based on the information, it seems that that she was married to an alcoholic or had an alcoholic father.

3 She points this out to show that Nation's behavior was not typical of the Temperance Movement.

## ◈ Planning                                          p.146

**Main Idea:** *Women were the main force in the Temperance Movement.*

Supporting Detail 1: *radicals – Carrie Nation, axe*

Supporting Detail 2: *mainstream – protests*

## ◈ Grading                                          p.146

**Sample Response**                                   02-94

The American Temperance Movement began in the late 1700s as a way to discourage the drinking of alcohol. Over time, the movement grew and took on more and more followers until it had the power to cause Prohibition in the United States. This was done in great part with the help of women. The professor discusses two types of female temperance supporters to argue her point. The first type she mentions is that of radicals. She explains this by using the example of Carrie Nation, who stormed into taverns with rocks and axes and destroyed interior decorations and kegs. But most of the women in the movement were not as aggressive as her. They supported the movement by teaching their children not to drink, and sometimes they held protests in front of taverns. In this way, women were the driving force behind the American Temperance Movement.

Chapter **12** | Integrated Speaking

## Task 4 | **Health: Diabetes**

## ◈ Listening                                          p.147

Script 02-95

**Professor:** Continuing our discussion about major health issues facing Americans today, I'd like to talk a bit now about diabetes. This is a condition that everyone has heard of but usually knows very

little about. So let me start by, ah, just giving you an overview of it. Basically, think of it like this: We eat food that has glucose, which our bodies turn into energy with a hormone called insulin. If someone has diabetes, that person's body cannot perform this function because of insulin problems.

I'll explain this a little further by describing the two major variations of diabetes, which are very simply named Type 1 and Type 2. With Type 1 diabetes, a person's pancreas produces little to no insulin. Type 1 diabetes usually appears in a person early in life—before the age of thirty—and must be treated with insulin injections. Type 2 diabetes, which usually develops after the age of forty, involves insufficient or ineffective insulin production. What I mean by ineffective is that the body for some reason is unable to make use of the insulin provided by the pancreas. The primary treatment for Type 2 diabetes is an exercise and diet regimen although insulin shots may also be used.

Now that you understand what diabetes is, let's talk about its symptoms. Some of the symptoms of diabetes are easy to notice and can be early warning signs. Things like excessive hunger and thirst, fatigue, and rapid weight loss should signal to most people that it's time to visit the doctor. But there are a number of, well, I guess we could call them hidden symptoms because many people don't notice them as being abnormal. These include such things as blurry vision, numbness, the slow healing of cuts and scratches, and dry or itchy skin.

1 The professor organizes the lecture into two parts. The first part details the two main types of diabetes. The second part discusses the symptoms of diabetes.

2 The hidden symptoms are things that may not seem very unusual and so would not be suspected as symptoms of illness by most people.

## ◈ Planning                                          p.148

**Main Idea:** *diabetes description and symptoms*

Supporting Detail 1: *Type 1 = young people; insulin shots; Type 2 = older people; diet + insulin*

Supporting Detail 2: *hunter, thirst, fatigue, weight loss + hidden symptoms – blurry vision, numbness, slow healing, and dry, itchy skin*

The lecture is on the topic of diabetes, which the professor says is something many people do not have a good understanding of. The basic definition of diabetes is that someone has problems with insulin. The professor expands on the definition by describing the two main types of diabetes. Type 1 diabetes is usually found in younger people. It has to be treated with insulin injections. Type 2 diabetes develops later in life and happens because the pancreas does not produce enough insulin or the body can't use the insulin it makes. This can be treated through diet and exercise or with insulin shots. The professor then moves on to discuss the symptoms of diabetes, which are warning signs that someone has the condition. The professor divides the symptoms between noticeable symptoms and hidden symptoms. The first kind includes rapid weight loss, fatigue, and constant hunger and thirst. The hidden symptoms are things like itchy skin, blurry vision, and numbness.

# Part C
## Experiencing the TOEFL iBT Actual Tests

### ▤ Actual Test 01

**Task 1**       p.151

#### Sample Response

I believe it is important for students to be involved in extracurricular activities. To start with, extracurricular activities can help round out a person's development. If a student only studies all the time, that individual will not develop important physical or social skills. But participating in extracurricular activities, such as joining a club or playing a sport, can help a student learn to interact with others in a nonacademic environment and develop interests or hobbies that can enrich that person's life. In addition to self-improvement, extracurricular activities can increase one's chances of getting into a top university. Many universities ask students about their leadership positions, athletic involvement, and community service. Having an impressive list of extracurricular activities on one's application would only increase one's chances of acceptance.

**Task 2**       p.152

#### Listening       Script 03-03

M: You really enjoy living in Rosemary Hall, don't you? How do you feel about not being permitted to stay there again next year?

W: It's a pretty good dormitory, so I suppose it will be somewhat inconvenient for me if I can't stay there. But overall, I don't really mind.

M: Seriously? Why not?

W: First of all, I think having an all-freshman dorm is a positive thing. I mean, adjusting to college life isn't easy, especially when upperclassmen might be pressuring you into doing activities you don't want to. So first-year students will be able to get used to college life there better.

M: That's a good point.

W: Plus, think about it . . . The school is currently building two new dormitories.

M: What's so important about that?

W: They are going to be incredible places to live. And if most of the freshmen are living in Rosemary Hall, that means more upperclassmen like us will get to live in those new dorms. I'm going to apply to live in one of them. I can't wait.

## Sample Response

The speakers are having a conversation about an announcement regarding a change in plans for Rosemary Hall. Presently, it houses first-, second-, and third-year students, but starting in the fall semester, only freshmen will be permitted to live there. The woman expresses her support for this decision and gives two reasons for feeling that way. First, she believes that freshmen need a place where they can be away from upperclassmen. Older students sometimes pressure freshmen to do actions they don't want to, so freshmen can adjust to college better by having their own dormitory. Second, the woman remarks that two new dormitories are being constructed on campus. She points out that with many freshmen living in Rosemary Hall, she and the man will have a better opportunity to live in the new buildings. She states they will be great places to live, so she intends to apply to live in one of them.

## Task 3

p.154

### Listening

Script 03-04

Professor: Measuring worker productivity isn't as easy as simply making some changes and crunching numbers. I'll explain what I mean. Have you ever heard of the Hawthorne Effect? Well, in a factory in the 1920s, researchers monitored workers who assembled telephones. They secretly monitored the workers' output levels for five years. Then they started making some changes: shortening the length of the working day, giving five- or ten-minute breaks at various intervals, changing salaries based on output, separating workers into private rooms, and on and on.

Now, each of these changes affected productivity. The researchers drew tentative conclusions about the perfect duration and occurrence of breaks, for example, based on these changes. They hypothesized that changes in the workplace affect worker productivity.

A later analysis of the study, however, revealed that nearly every change that was made increased worker productivity. How was this possible? As it turns out, productivity increased simply because the test subjects knew they were being observed. So the Hawthorne Effect refers to this self-modified behavior rather than the preliminary findings of the study. It really demonstrates to us the difficulty of measuring worker productivity.

## Sample Response

The Hawthorne Effect describes the phenomenon of workers increasing their own productivity when they know that they're being watched. The effect was noticed after a five-year study done on workers in a factory. There, researchers began to change various things in the workers' environment, such as their work schedules, break times, and management and the physical surroundings in the factory. Each change brought about increased productivity among workers, so the first assumptions were that the changes themselves were responsible for the higher output levels. The professor explains that this was not actually the case though. After analyzing the results of the study further, researchers finally concluded that it was not the changes that increased productivity, but rather the fact that the workers knew they were being monitored. The professor explains that this, the Hawthorne Effect, makes it difficult to measure worker productivity.

## Task 4

p.156

### Listening

Script 03-05

Professor: Let's take a moment now to talk about the ways that humans use animals for our own purposes. Animals that are trained to perform specific tasks for us are loosely categorized as working animals. The way we use working animals greatly depends on each animal's individual attributes.

The oldest way that humans have been using animals is by training them to be draft animals. These are large, strong animals that are used by us for their strength and are trained to perform heavy labor tasks. For millennia, we humans have used camels to carry heavy loads through the desert, oxen to plow the fields, and horses to pull carts or wagons. While industrialized nations today have done away with the use of draft animals by and large, they are still depended on by millions of people living in non-industrialized countries or regions of farmland that cannot support modern equipment.

Another highly visible type of working animal is the service animal. These animals are trained to help humans because of their intelligence, natural senses, and instincts. I'm sure we've all seen guide dogs leading around someone who is vision impaired. Guide dogs are able to lead people safely down the street and can even protect them from danger. Another service animal is the monkey. That's right, folks. Monkeys can be trained to help those who have been injured and have mobility problems. Helper monkeys can do things like wash a person's face, turn the pages of a magazine, and even microwave food.

## Sample Response

Working animals are animals that are trained and used by humans to do tasks for us. The professor explains this concept by defining two categories of working animals. The first category is draft animals. The professor states that draft animals are chosen by humans because of their strength. There are various animals, such as oxen and camels, that can pull carts or plow fields on a farm. These animals are seldom used in modern societies but are still instrumental in the development of some civilizations. The other category of working animal described by the professor is that of service animals. Service animals are trained to help humans with disabilities do daily tasks. One example given of a service animal is the guide dog, which helps people with vision impairments find their way around. The other example is of helper monkeys, which do basic tasks around the house for people who have problems with mobility.

#  Actual Test 02

## Task 1
p.159

### Sample Response

I agree that to understand another country's culture, you must first understand its language. First, one of the best ways to learn a country's culture is to watch its television programs and movies. My older brother lived in Spain and learned the language. He loved watching Spanish TV programs and movies. He said he learned very much about Spanish culture from watching them thanks to his language skills. Second, understanding another language lets you read literature in its original language. You can then gain a deeper understanding of the people and their culture. Again, my brother loved Spanish literature, especially novels and poems. Reading them in Spanish helped him understand how the people of Spain think, and that improved his knowledge of Spanish culture very much.

## Task 2
p.160

### Listening
Script 03-08

M: Whoa, check this out, Sarah! All right! I was tired of that old laundry room we had to use.

W: Hmm, let me see . . . Oh, gosh. A fifty-cent increase in the price? That's really drastic.

M: But the price per pound is the same. You can shove more clothes in the washer and get the same value.

W: Who on earth washes twenty pounds of clothes at a time? I sure don't. I wouldn't even be able to carry that many. My wash loads will, of course, stay the same, but now I'm going to have to pay an extra fifty cents. This is obscene.

M: Well, maybe you have a point. At least it's a new facility though. The old one was getting run down.

W: Old or not, I'd rather go with the cheaper option. Besides, the current laundry room is in the basement of my dorm building. Now I'm going to have to walk all the way to Perkins every time I need to wash my clothes.

M: Hey, it's not like the extra exercise is going to kill you.

### Sample Response

The students are talking about an announcement about a new laundry facility. The new facility has bigger machines that handle larger loads of laundry at a higher cost. The woman is unhappy about the announcement, and she mentions a couple of reasons why. Her first reason is that she does not appreciate the higher price. She says that even though the washing machines hold twenty pounds, she will not be able to benefit from it because she doesn't wash that many clothes at one time. Thus, she's upset about the additional fifty cents for doing a load of laundry. Her second reason is that she doesn't like the location of the new facility. The existing laundry facility is in the basement of her dormitory building, but the new facility will require her to walk to another building. So she wishes the existing laundry facility would not be shut down.

## Task 3
p.162

### Listening
Script 03-09

Professor: Good morning, everyone. Today, we're going to pick up where we left off in the last lecture. If you recall, I introduced you to the concept of logical fallacies and gave you an overview of a few of them. Today, I'd like to go into more detail with a few of them, starting with the fallacy known as the strawman.

You may not have heard this term before, but you'll definitely recognize what it is when I tell you. A strawman is when you take someone's argument, twist it around so that it says something that's easier to attack, and then argue against your new representation of the person's argument. I know that's a lot to digest, so let me put this in more concrete terms. Let's say that Politician A argues that we should reduce the country's budget by changing the way public education is funded. Politician B responds by saying, "I can't believe that Politician A wants to get rid of public education! He is against children!" In this case, Politician B has changed Politician A's argument. It has been distorted so that Politician B can easily attack it. That's what a strawman is, and it actually happens quite frequently.

## Sample Response

A logical fallacy is a problem with an argument that can cause confusion or even invalidate the argument. The professor illustrates the concept of logical fallacies by explaining the example of the strawman fallacy. This occurs when someone misrepresents an opponent's argument in a way that makes it easier to attack. The professor uses an example of two politicians to clarify what the strawman fallacy is. If one politician proposes changes to the education system, another politician might argue that his opponent wants to cut education funding from the public budget. This is obviously not what the first politician proposed, but misrepresenting the proposition allows the second politician to argue from a more secure position. So the example of the politicians illustrates the strawman fallacy and helps explain why logical fallacies are important in philosophy and logic.

## Task 4

p.164

### Listening

Script 03-10

**Professor:** Why did you come to class today? Why did you put on clean clothes? For those with part-time jobs, why do you go to work after a long day of studying? Really, why do we humans do anything at all? The answer, simply put, is motivation. Everything we do happens because we were motivated somehow. It's a pretty complex issue, motivation . . . but for today we'll just talk about the broader categories of intrinsic and extrinsic motivation. Sounds simple, right?

Now, intrinsic motivation, as the name suggests, is something inside us that helps us motivate ourselves. This usually means that we gain some kind of satisfaction or enjoyment out of the activity. To illustrate this concept, think about the way that people pursue hobbies. Someone might spend an entire weekend enthusiastically searching for and organizing rare coins. There's no measurable benefit to, um, to collecting coins, but it's something that brings this person happiness.

So it should be pretty clear now what extrinsic motivation is. Yep, that's right: rewards and punishments brought on by outside forces. I asked you earlier why you came to class. Well, I'd wager that many of you came to avoid having points taken off your final grade in the class. That's a perfect example of an extrinsic

reward. You didn't come to class today because you find such great pleasure in hearing me talk about psychology; you came because you were motivated by the threat of a lower final grade in the class.

## Sample Response

According to the lecture, everything that we do is because we were motivated in some way to act. The professor explains that there are two types of motivation. The first type is called intrinsic motivation. This is the type of motivation that we can find within ourselves, usually because we enjoy an activity. The professor uses the example of collecting coins. To someone who enjoys that hobby, it would be easy to spend all weekend organizing their coins because it would bring them happiness to do so. This is intrinsic motivation. The other type of motivation is called extrinsic motivation, and it is easily understood as being rewards and punishments. The professor explains that students probably attend a class not because they find happiness in listening to a lecture but because they don't want to be penalized in their final grade. This illustrates how external factors can motivate us to act.

# TOEFL®
# MAP New TOEFL® Edition
## Speaking

Advanced